Skira Architecture Library

5+1

The shadow of ideas

Edited by
Sebastiano Brandolini

Photographs by
Ernesta Caviola

Skira

Editor
Luca Molinari

Editing
Anna Albano
Lidia Maurizi

Layout
Paola Ranzini

English translation
Tim Stroud

First published in Italy
in 2001 by
Skira Editore S.p.A.
Palazzo Casati Stampa
via Torino 61
20123 Milano
Italy

Printed and bound in Italy.
First edition

ISBN 88-8118-910-0

Distributed in North
America and Latin America
by Abbeville Publishing
Group, 22 Cortlandt Street,
New York, NY 10007, USA..
Distributed elsewhere in the
world by Thames and
Hudson Ltd., 181a High
Holborn, London WC1V
7QX, United Kingdom.

This volume is published to coincide with the exhibition
5+1 architetti associati, Genua
12 January - 22 March 2001
GTA (Institut für Geschichte und Theorie der Architektur)
Departement Architektur der ETH, Zurich; ARchENA;
ETH Hönggerberg

Board of the Institute
Werner Oechslin, director
Vittorio Magnago Lampugnani

Project manager
Philippe Carrard, GTA exhibition manager

5+1 extend particular thanks to
the GTA of the ETH, Zurich
Sebastiano Brandolini, Rudy Ricciotti, Yves Nacher,
Maurizio Giufré for their co-operation
Philippe Chaix, Brunetto De Batté, Francesco Guerisoli,
Alessandro Schiesaro, Giuseppe Vagge for their appreciation
and friendship
Enrico D. Bona with affection for the time we have spent
together
Luca Molinari for the enthusiasm with which
he has received our work

gta Eidgenössische Technische Hochschule Zürich
Institut für Geschichte und Theorie der Architektur

+

Contents

In the shadow of ideas: haste

There are no masters in the shadow of ideas, only fellow-sufferers.
Everything is clearer in the shadow of ideas: in the absence of fathers to stab in the back, one has to act with will and determination.
In the shadows, movements are quicker, like reflexes of the senses. The project is built up with a series of rapid decisions, decisions that should never be pondered over. Haste is the essence as work is the crux of daily life. Haste is a necessary condition that is itself only conditioned by how things are going.
Staying in the shadow of ideas is a political, combative stance, not one of resignation because here you can strike better, more effectively and with greater menace.
But what can you do?
Try and make sense of the shadows we pass through each day.
Emotions form our will-power.
Ideas slap or caress with the palm of the hand, never with the back.
Shadows show you how things really are and highlight the differences. Shadows are a clearing in perception.

Rudy Ricciotti

5 penguins+one

Five penguins in profile and one head on, what an odd image to represent an architectural agency.

We can't really be talking about a group of those large, flat-footed marine birds with white and black feathers that live in the Arctic, can we? After all, it would be utterly wrong to consider the lovely city of Genoa in north Italy as cold as the Pole.

What they do have in common, though, is that the architects certainly have the same plumage as their colleagues in the Arctic. No natural protection, no armoured skin, but discretion and an amusing and disquieting gaze that makes those geographically distant birds seem so quaint.

In whatever order you meet Paola, Pierluigi, Alfonso, Gianluca and Maurizio, there is always the feeling of a united family, it's almost exasperating. Surely they argue amongst themselves?

The comparison with the large, charming and excessively social penguins stops right there.

In Savona, brutality versus banality, the gentle bird struck hard with a heavyweight blow to the chin using its long, radical reach. The mass of archaic stone blocks that runs parallel to the sea introduces an unambiguous attitude: the architect is on the side of the sea rather than that of the city. Their courageous, non-consensual choice (they could have chosen to be minimalist like the children of good families that they are) dragged them into their first political argument: in an unexpected move during the election campaign, the Left exploited the project and made the sign of the cross you would normally use to ward off a vampire.

And so a new urban area was created by the artificial barrier laid right in the city. The beaches are divided from the standard city noise to produce a protected, wild, intimate and romantic environment remote from the urban culture. There is no polished granite, no obsequious stainless steel, no flattering aluminium: here there is nothing but stones, bits of wood, rugged palm trees and sand.

In complete contrast, at Sestri Levante these tough penguins threw themselves unhesitatingly and hallucenogenically into the kind of project where so many aspiring young architects have failed before, the organisation of a roundabout right in the city centre. Having neatly wrapped up all the loose ends, the rockers decided to add a light touch to the practicality — prohibited of course — proposing to plant a hundred or so artificial sunflowers topped by a hundred plastic doves. This idea of genius, however, was frowned upon by the city council and now the roundabout is nothing but a green disc.

At Celle Ligure, vulgarity versus cynicism, the five penguins had an ugly encounter with your butler. From this unfinished project a degree of remorse arose; having lost their natural elegance, the penguins abandoned themselves to the bottle and hooliganism. They lit up the street with the help of Federico Fellini, they built the largest bench in Italy and, without any feelings of conscience, they expanded on the patches of greenery planted haphazardly by shop-owners. It was a eulogy to vulgarity, the placing in authority of an uncultured landscape architect and the revelation that wine affects the brain.

Fornaci promenade, Savona

Savona City Council
Schedule: organisation of the promenade along Corso Vittorio Veneto
Length: 1 km
Costs: 1.3 billion lire
Period: 1996–98

The surrounding city is fortunate in the quality of its natural environment (it has a long and deep shoreline) but it has been built in the unimaginative, discontinuous manner that is typical of Italy since 1945. The decision was made to take a stance against this banality by the inclusion of the tango steps on the bridge, by increasing the number of public facilities (seats, pergolas, walkways on the beach), and by deforming various elements of the street furniture (the rocks, the appalling 1950's buildings, the bus stop as long as the bus itself and an insult to Italian urban furniture, the children's play area like houses, the shelter for card-players like in a western).

Continuous and discontinuous lines of vision
Don't allow the pedestrian unbroken views but continuous breaks to the side (even short ones) to force him to turn and experience his environment; nor allow him long flat stretches but provide changes in slope to vary his position in space.

Greenery
The relationship between the unplanned pattern in which the trees were planted in the past and the regularity of the new arrangement was exploited. A play area was given much more scope by making it attractive also to older children by, for example, providing special skateboarding facilities.

View from passing cars
The desire to visit the new area is also stimulated by the view one has of it from a passing car. Although the area had to be protected from the road, it was necessary to allow the motorist to catch attractive glimpses of it that kindle his interest.
The sea is better
Unbelievably, the previous promenade gave priority to the view of the city and the cars rather than that of the beach and sea and the activities taking place on them. The project reversed the situation placing emphasis on the natural rather than the artificial, sometimes descending to the level of the beach, sometimes rising to give a panoramic view.

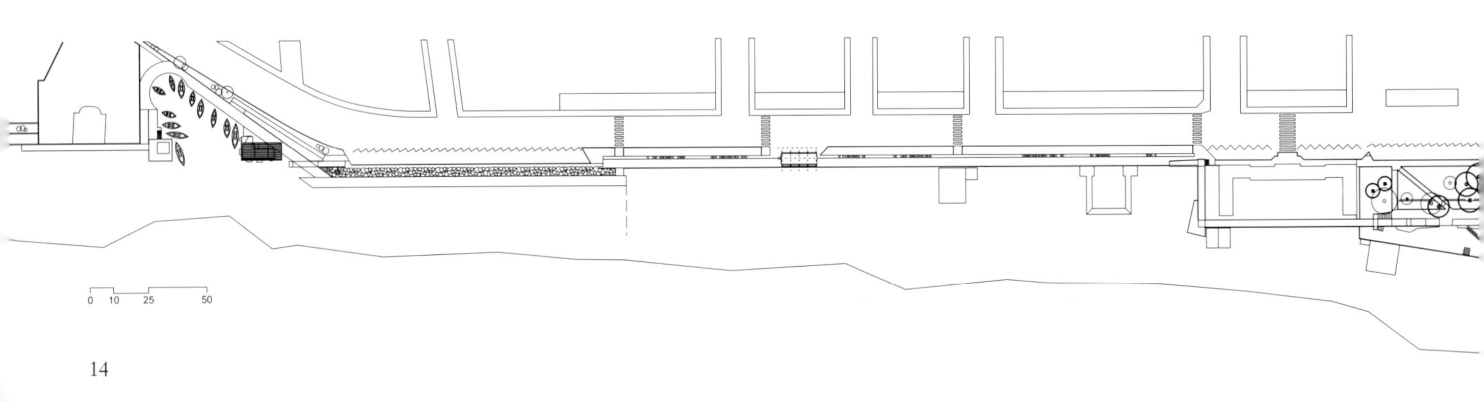

Plan

Project layout
1. Wooden walkways
2. Walkways
3. Greenery
4. Views

Next page:
Tango steps: in admiration of Carlos Gardel

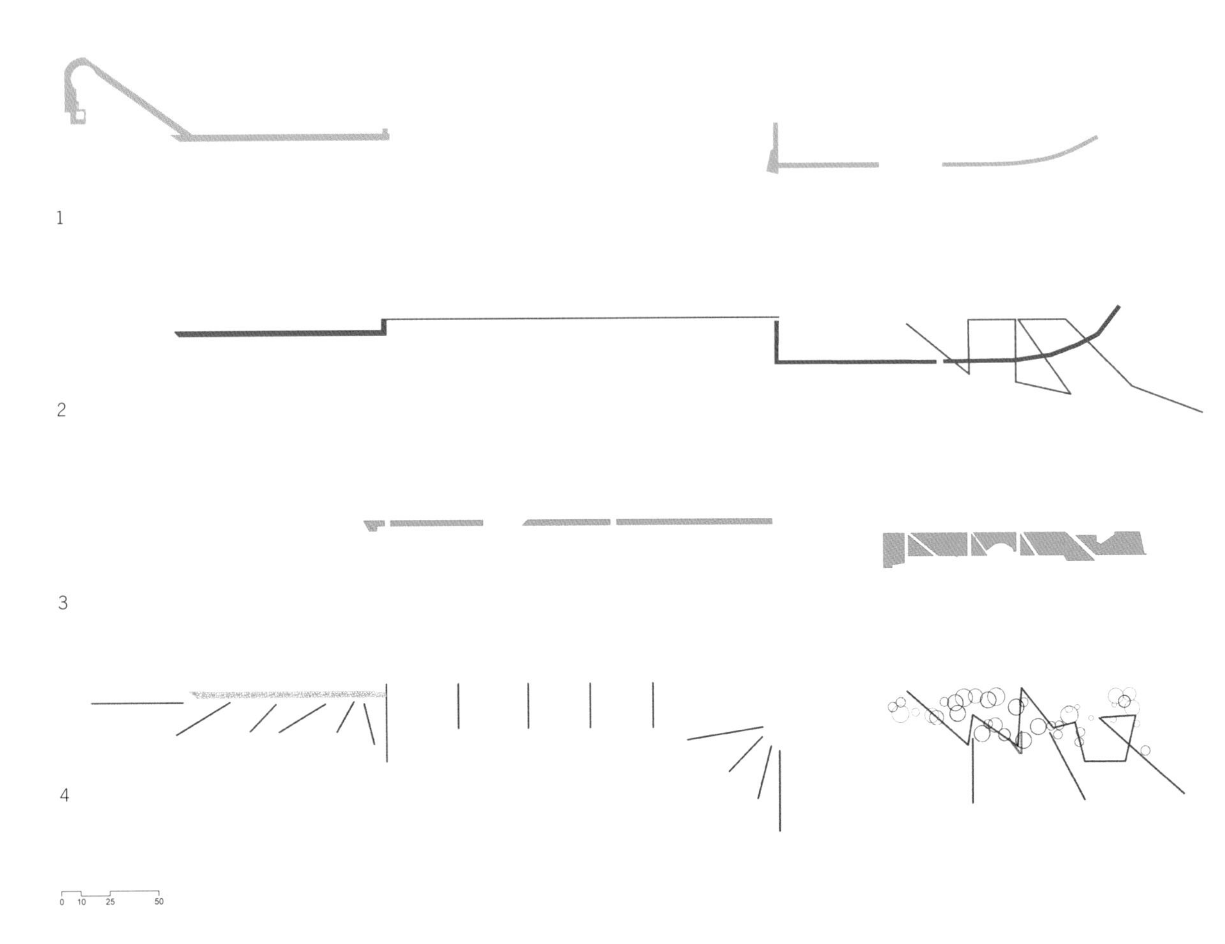

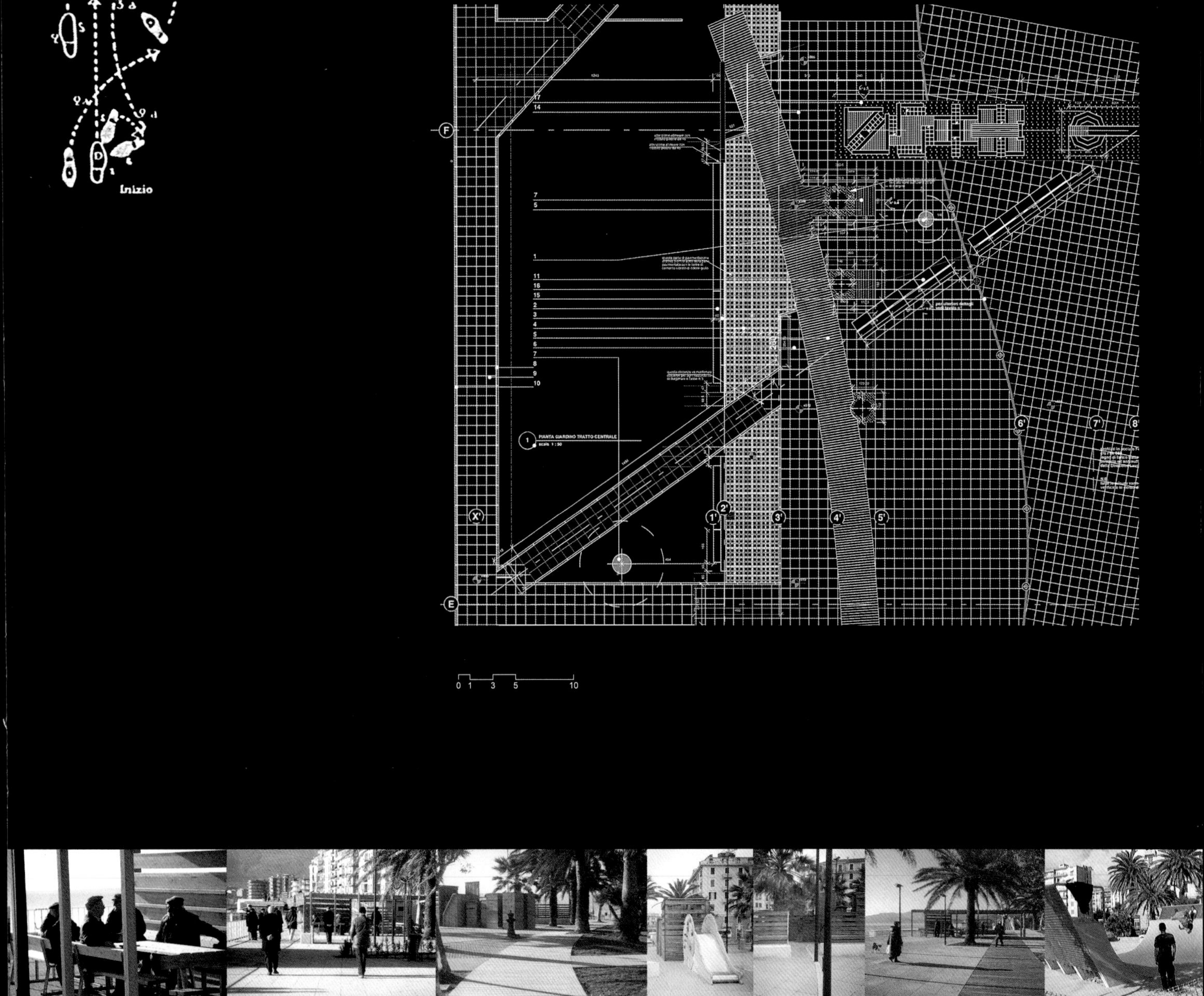
Inizio
PIANTA GIARDINO TRATTO CENTRALE
scala 1 : 50
0 1 3 5 10

The walkway descends
to beach level

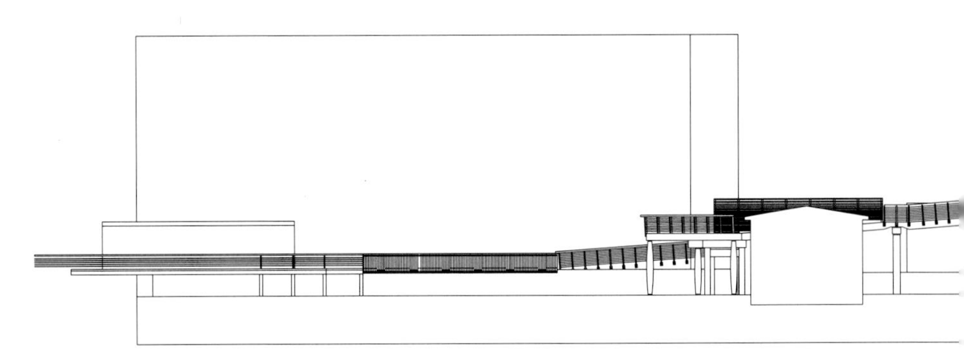

A system of raised walkways and platforms looks over the interruptions

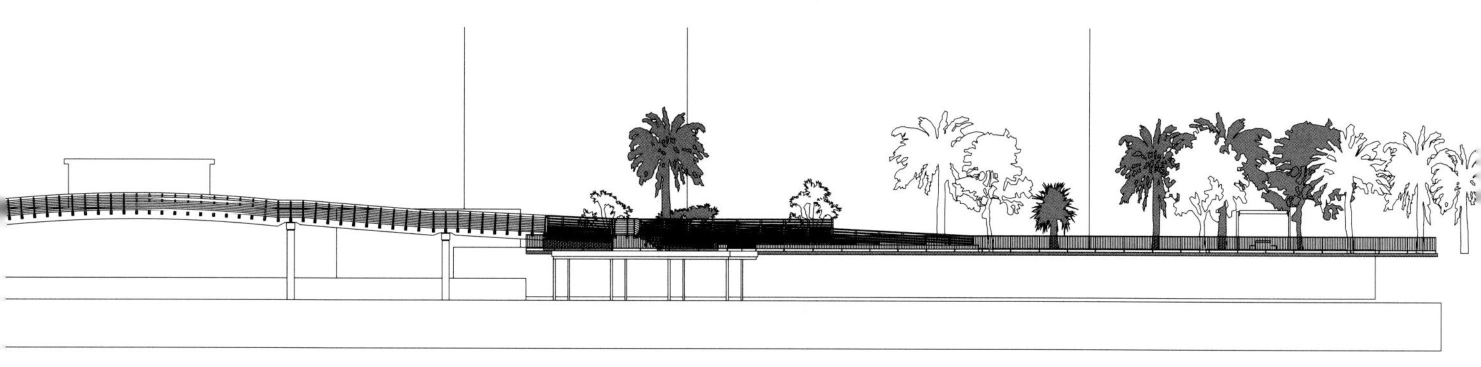

The gardens

Following pages:
The bus stop

The play area

geometry as **contrast**

Piazza Sant'Antonio, Sestri Levante

Sestri Levante City Council
Schedule: organisation of Piazza Sant'Antonio
Area: 2600 sqm
Cost: 900 million lire
Period: 1996–99

'Where the historical centre meets the buildings of the twentieth century expansion of the city, there is a sequence of three squares in the space of a few dozen metres that marks the entrance to and exit from the city. It is an irony of fate that these two fringes are visible to the visitor crossing Sestri Levante along Via Aurelia.

As the car driver's perception of his surroundings needs to be so much more rapid than that of a pedestrian, maybe the areas that are currently no more than semi-chaotic vehicle junctions should be re-organised so that the slower and more complex movements of the pedestrians should condition the movements of the traffic.

The Via Aurelia divides the city into two sections that might be summarised as the territories of the pedestrian and the car. The aim of the project was to ratify the two territories within the two areas.

A circle and a line are the "images" that epitomise the work done. The circle over Piazza Sant'Antonio re-establishes the strong dissimilarity of the fronts facing onto the square and concentrates, in one point, on the image of the entrance, highlighting the "negative" spaces of the church square, the gardens and the entrance to the historical centre. The line connects the extension of Via Dante to Via Nazionale cutting the egg of the roundabout in Piazza della Repubblica and projecting the city towards the nearby countryside. The images should of course be inverted if one is coming from the other direction.

The trees and natural decoration are not simply used to prettify the roads but as colour that changes with the seasons'.

Enrico D. Bona

Aerial view of the area
before the project

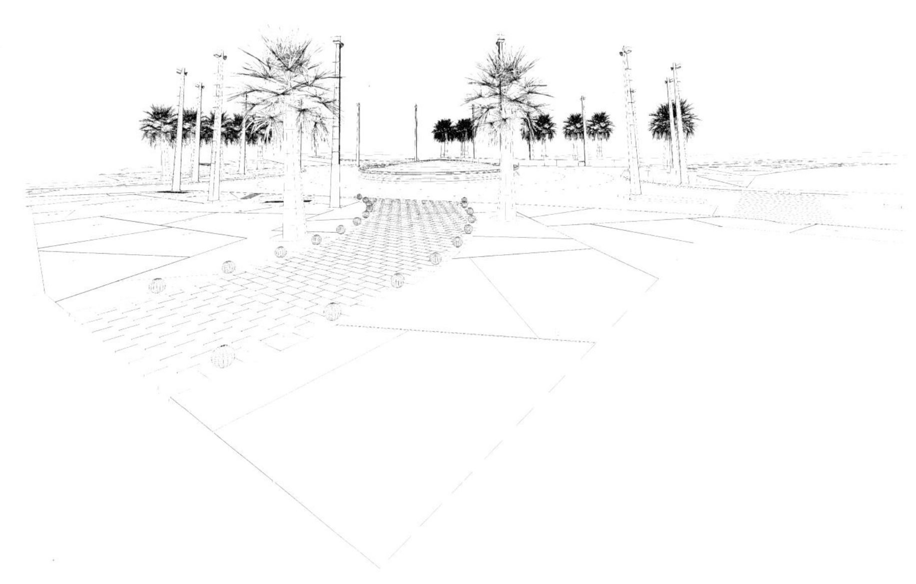

The roundabout:
two plans compared

Next page:
the elements of the
project: concrete, glass
bricks, stone, light,
wood, plants

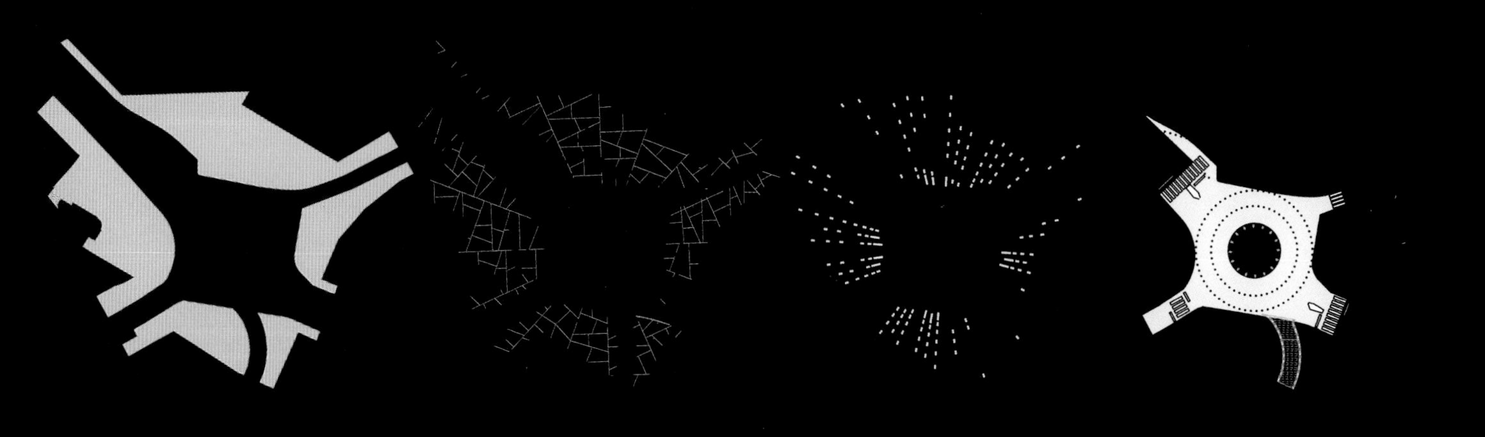

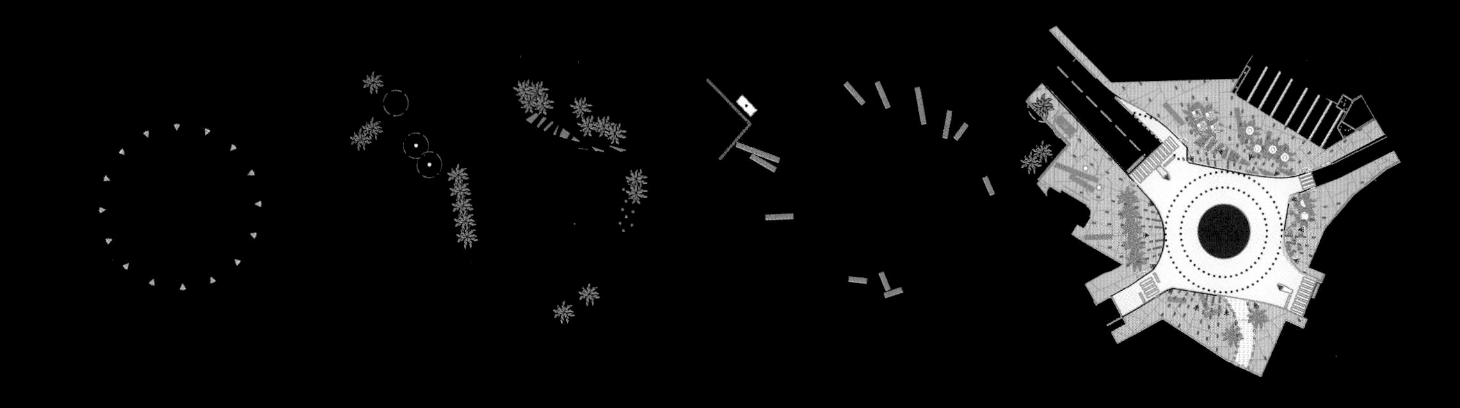

Strollers in the square

Montage of the second roundabout plan

Viale Dante, Sestri Levante

Sestri Levante City Council
Schedule: reorganisation of Viale Dante
Extension: 2400 sqm
Cost: 500 million lire
Period: 1996–99

The pedestrian route was extended asymmetrically with direct and indirect lighting and a pavement/square was created in front of the school.

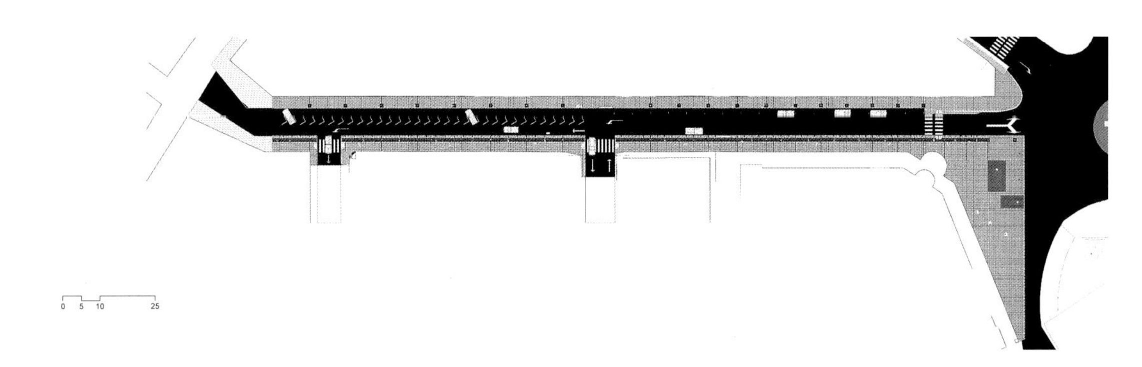

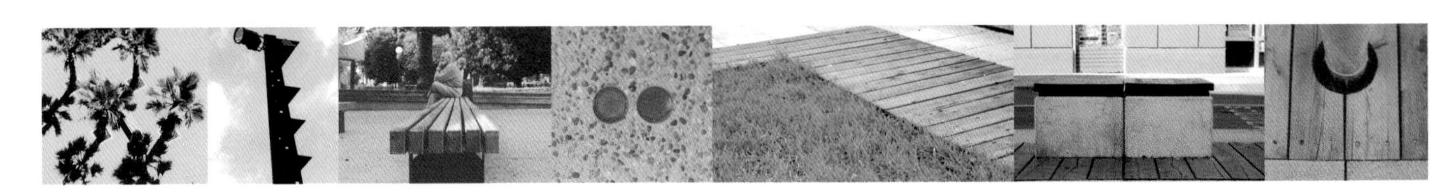

BANCA
CARAMILLA

vulgarity versus **cynicism**

Piazza dell'Assunta and Via Genova, Celle Ligure

Celle Ligure City Council
Schedule: reorganisation of Piazza dell'Assunta, Via Genova and the seafront
Cost: 800 million lire
Period: 1997 - in progress

The aim of the project was to create some form of contact with the rather vulgar 1960s buildings in the tourist area of the city, not by lowering the project to the taste of the garden gnome set, but by using materials reminiscent of the private, family environment (plants and trees, light, images of the *Dolce vita* and memories) which were the basic components used in the indiscriminate shoreline construction over the last half century. No nostalgia, however: the district has no local centre (Piazza dell'Assunta is a desert) and the busy junction with Via Aurelia is only for vehicles which means that one part of the city is effectively blocked off.

The tall palm trees are a noble, natural monument that give the square the geometry it so badly needs. Around the edge of the square, a continuous green border matches the existing vulgar growth of olive trees, oleanders, pines and dragon trees which have been maintained as they are. Along Via Genova it was sufficient to bound the area reserved for pedestrians with a material unsuitable to vehicles that stretches down to the promenade area where the view opens out to the horizon.

The pedestrian crossing has been made safe and the entrance to the district given a strong identification through lighting and paving; a square has been illuminated by suspended industrial lighting and a wooden enclosure created beneath the pines where coloured, revolving seats have been installed. The perimeter with existing flowerbeds has been given a long wooden bench that faces towards the sea.

Here too 'deformation' and 'virile ambiguity' are the common denominators of the series of objects: coloured revolving seats that are half barber's seat and half children's toys (who are their greatest users), an absurdly long and high bench along the promenade that can be used for a daytime snooze, and the suspended industrial lighting that seems to be a blend of village fête, the wedding in *Amarcord*, street lighting and a bowls club.

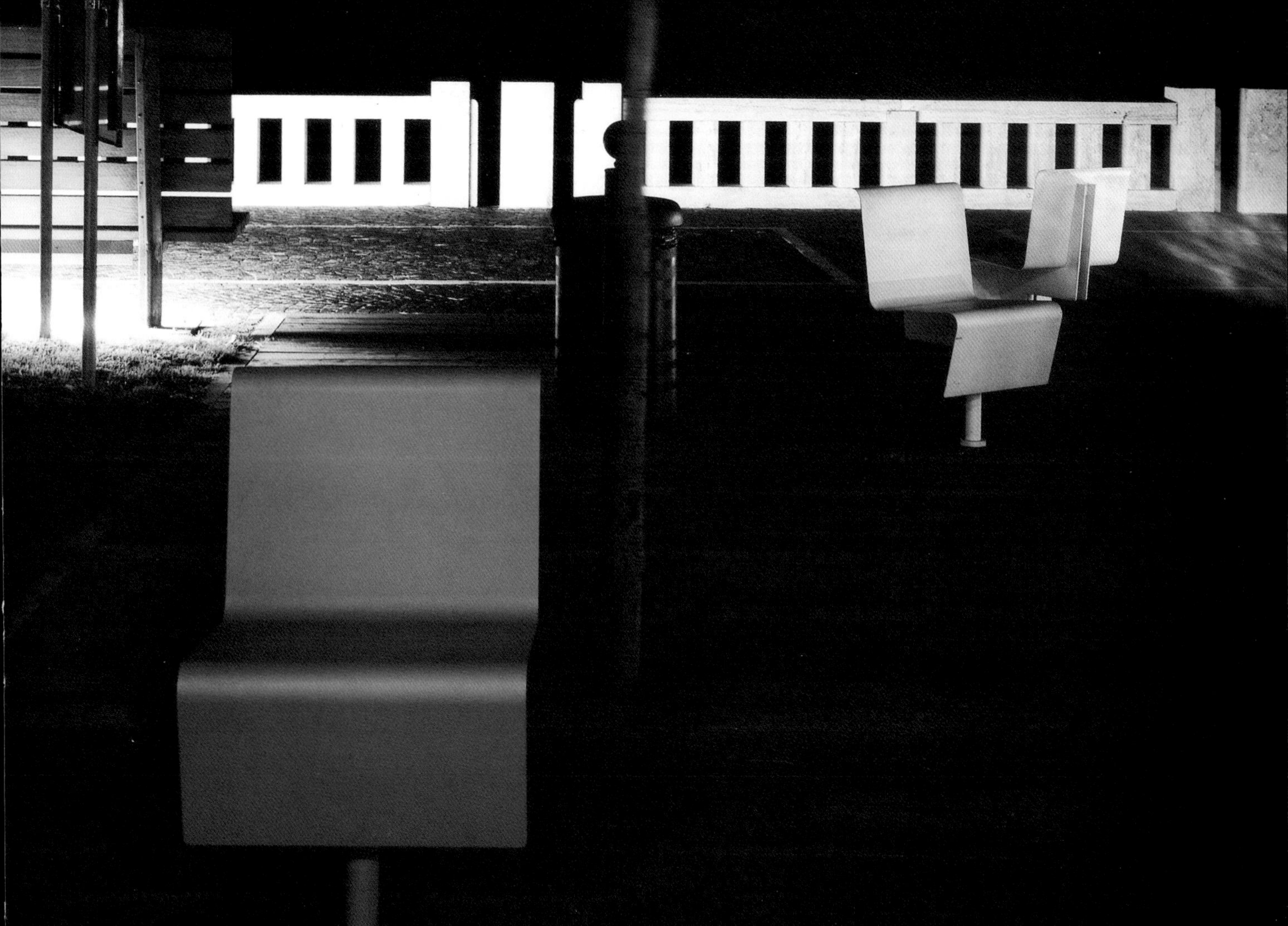

HOTEL

1
2
4
0
5
10
25

Plan:
1. Piazza dell'Assunta
2. Via Genova
3. Via Aurelia
4. Seafront promenade

It's better not to remember

It's better not to remember.
It's better to let thought deform reality in order to adapt it to that nebulous form that remains imagination.
Images materialise that were thought lost for ever. Other ideas are engaged having been stimulated by these chance encounters.
It's better to let memories merge and blend, as occurs during those moments as you wake, when you try to recall your fading dreams and, using invention or logic, to fill the gaps where, unrestricted by consciousness, your mind drifts towards the absurd and unreal.
You look for images by flicking through books and magazines or by digging into your fleeting, weakened memories. You're searching for a sensation, a space, a sequence of colours, a special material whether it was shiny, rough, wrinkled, almost metallic or iridescent.

Maurizio Giufré

The state of things

In nature, neither colour nor lines exist: there is nothing but sunshine and shadow...
Francisco Goya y Lucientes

In the context of 5+1's output, the university campus in Savona and the Antiquarium in Aquileia are both important examples of projects based on existing sites despite being in utterly different contexts and having dissimilar origins. Both are confirmation of the attitude — already seen in their brand new projects — taken by the architects from Liguria of laying down clear game-rules in a process to give meaning to the mass of signs (whether permanent or varying) that make up an architectural form. This process disregards all a priori stylistic definitions and what Jean Nouvel described as 'connecting new expressions of the vocabulary with older, more archaic words in order to give them as much sense, synergy and dynamism as possible'.[1]

Building a dialectic between the various elements in the overall composition is also 5+1's aim and, to do that, one of the first tasks is to reduce to the minimum, 'choosing only what is necessary'. This refers to the selection of the techniques and the materials to be used to simplify and make the composition recognisable. That does not mean following a path of abstract minimalism or the 'ultra-simplicity' of much architecture abroad. The search for the 'essential' must also provide for the 'exception' that always appears even in a modest architectural element but which assumes greater importance in the outstanding circumstances of an existing site and in exceptions to the norm (as in the two above-mentioned projects).

Constraints deriving from the existence of military buildings like the former Bligny Barracks or the archaeological ruins of a Roman basilica or *macellum* are the 'dynamic materials' to be used on the project, in the words of Rudy Ricciotti, an architect with whom 5+1 have shared many cultural adventures. These materials have a positive influence on any work and contribute to the final aim of enriching the building but of simultaneously achieving the 'plurality of forms' by means of a 'uniformity of method' that has always been important to modernity.[2]

In Savona, as in Aquileia, what was left and reused were the volumes and the structures on which a complex 'transmutation' was performed.[3] What occurred was a morphological transformation of the existing structures that architecture made visible by endowing the actual with new meanings. Thus, in Savona university campus — an authentic *Stadtkrone*, reminding of Taut — the system of *brise-soleil* that overlays the military buildings creates a new urban landscape that incorporates the existing elements. The volumes have been perforated with large windows to usher in the light, and the irregular surface of the wooden flooring that connects the complex to the 'small building' alters the established routes and breaks the rigidity of the original layout.

In the Antiquarium, however, the presence of the archaeological site is enhanced by the zenithal view of the interior that opens above the excavations. The ventilated walls shut out the light, which is only able to enter through the large opening overhead (a reference to Italian Gothic architecture); from this vantage point and from the highest point on the outside steps, it is possible to survey the entire horizon.

Both projects share the knowledge that 'the pre-formed is soon re-transformed'[4] through a process of the redefinition of forms that continues through time. History does not 'become aphasic or turn into a personal whim'[5] as Manfredo Tafuri used to state, because the 'experience of contemporaneousness' is experienced critically and outside of any rhetorical or gratuitous formal exercise.

[1] Jean Nouvel, *Una lezione in Italia. Architettura e design 1976-1995*, pp. 12-13, Milan, 1996.
[2] Stanislaus von Moos, 'Recycling Max Bill', in *Minimal Tradition*, p. 17, Baden, Bern, Milan, 1996.
[3] For the concept of transmutation see: Dino Formaggio, *Estetica, tempo, progetto*, edited by E. D'Alfonso and E. Franzini, Milan 1990.
[4] *Ibidem*, p. 125.
[5] Manfredo Tafuri, 'Storia, conservazione, restauro', interviewed by Chiara Baglione and Bruno Pedretti, in *Casabella* n. 580, June 1991. Now in: AA.VV., *Il progetto del passato*, ed. by Bruno Pedretti, p. 100, Milan 1997.

division versus **typology**

Museum, visitor centre and the Antiquarium in Aquileia Forum

The Superintendency of Archaeology
and Art for Friuli-Venezia Giulia
Schedule: New Archaeological Museum
in Aquileia Forum
Surface area: 2000 sqm
Cost: 4.1 billion lire
Period: 1998–2000

The basis for the project was a series of intersecting reinforced concrete walls rather than a real building. The original project was to cover an excavation site with a building somewhat like a basilica in nature and which resembled old manufacturing buildings that still stand in the area. The aim was to lighten the composition by dividing the entire structure into three sections differentiated by type of material (plaster, brick and fibrocement) that matched the interior and exterior walkways.

The underlying idea is that the museum space should not be restricted to the two open space floors of the building itself but include the area surrounding the building. For this reason, the south face has been given a large window that faces the ancient *macellum*, visible from almost all the building, and an outdoor stairway (west side) has been built as an observatory of the site so that ongoing excavations can be monitored; the stairway also functions as an outdoor walkway that goes as far as the foundations of the ancient huts.

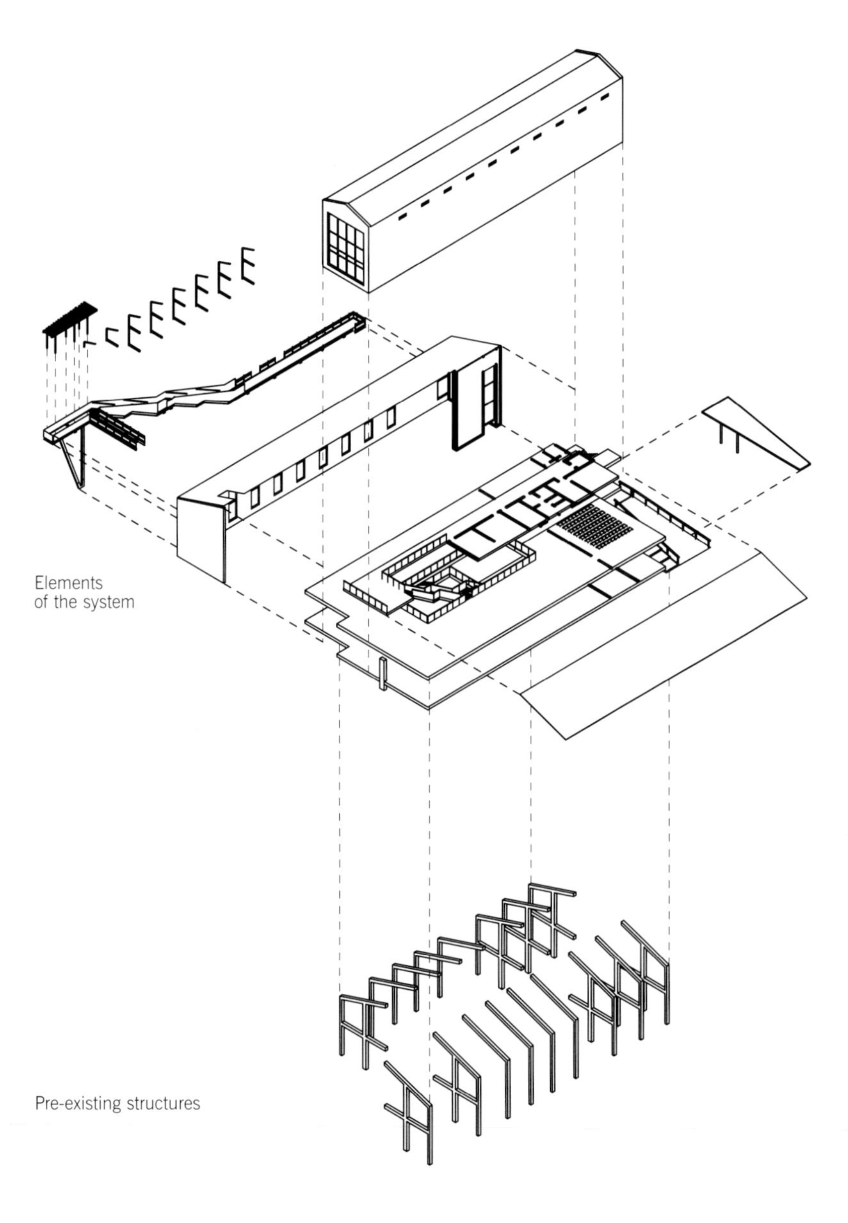
Elements
of the system
Pre-existing structures

Ground floor plan

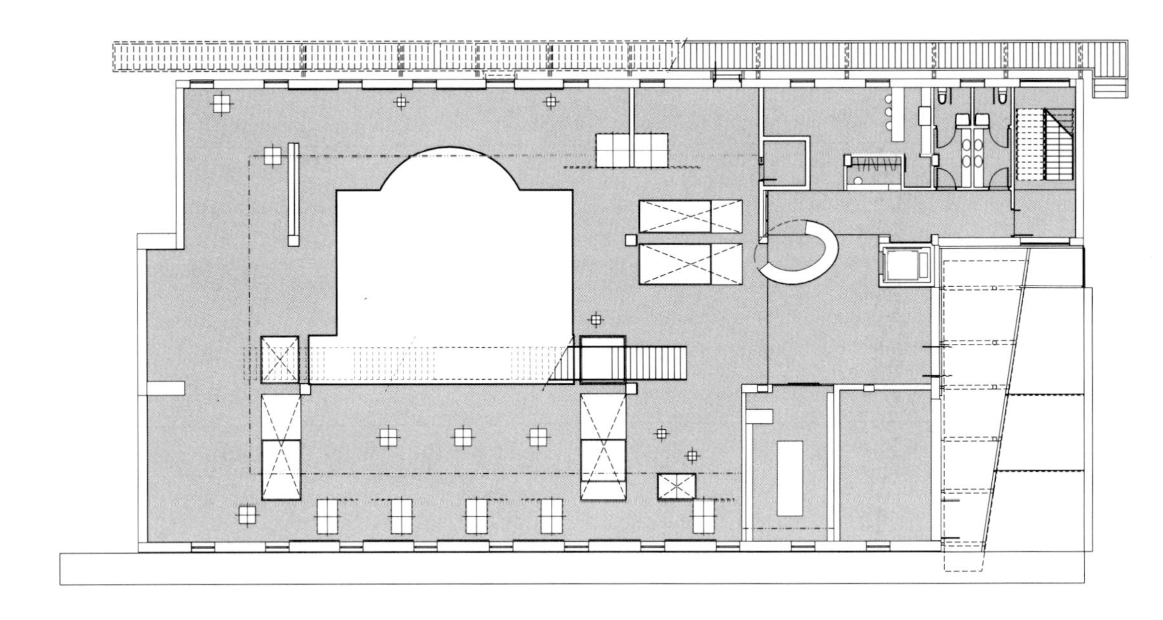

0 1 2 5

First floor plan

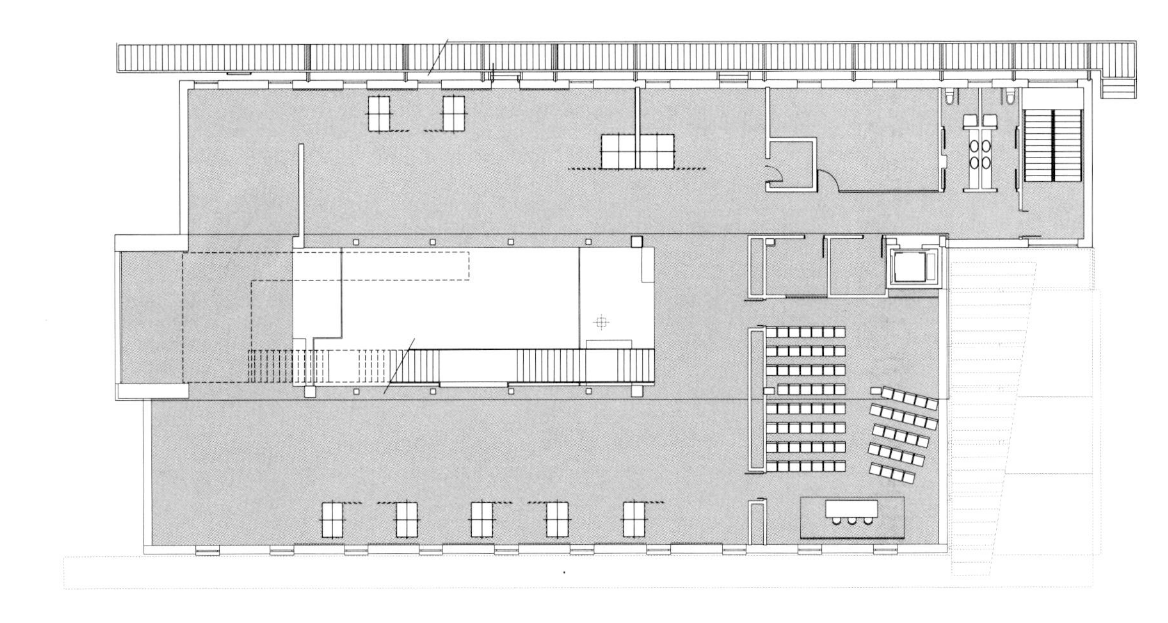

East elevation

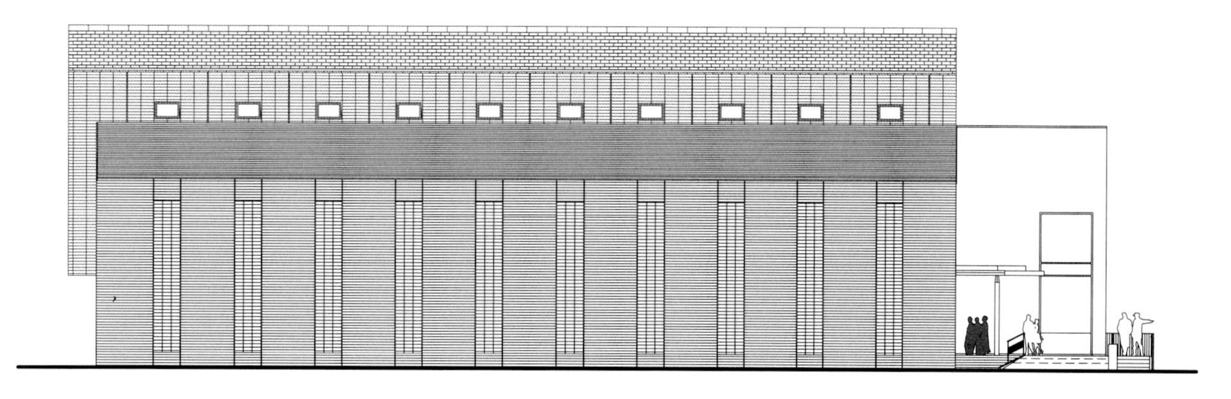

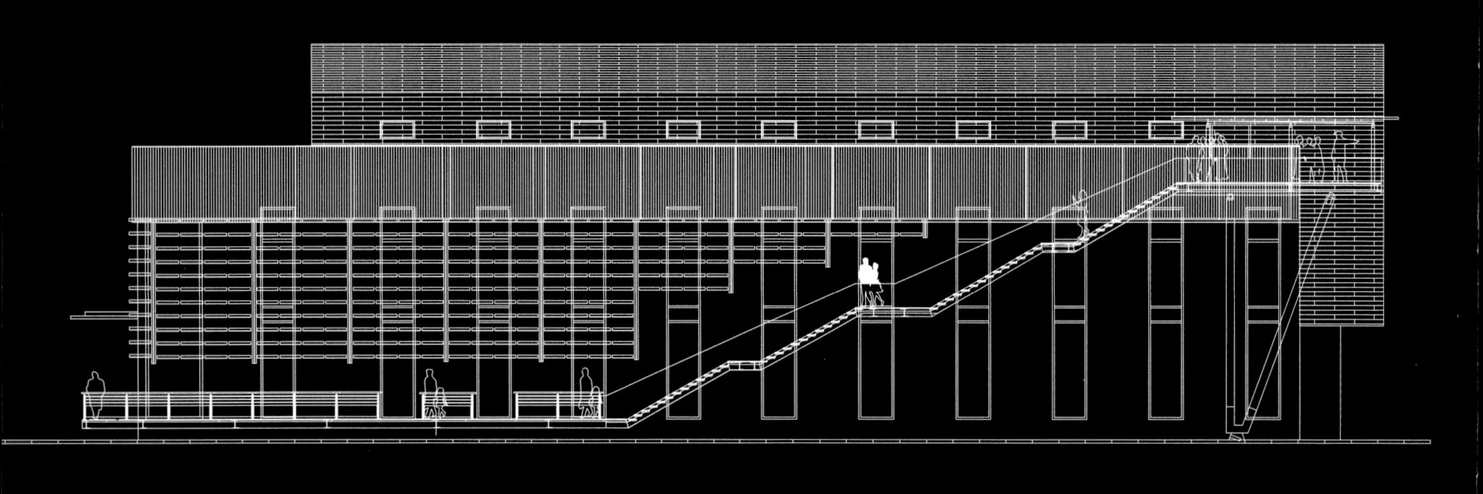
0 1 2 5

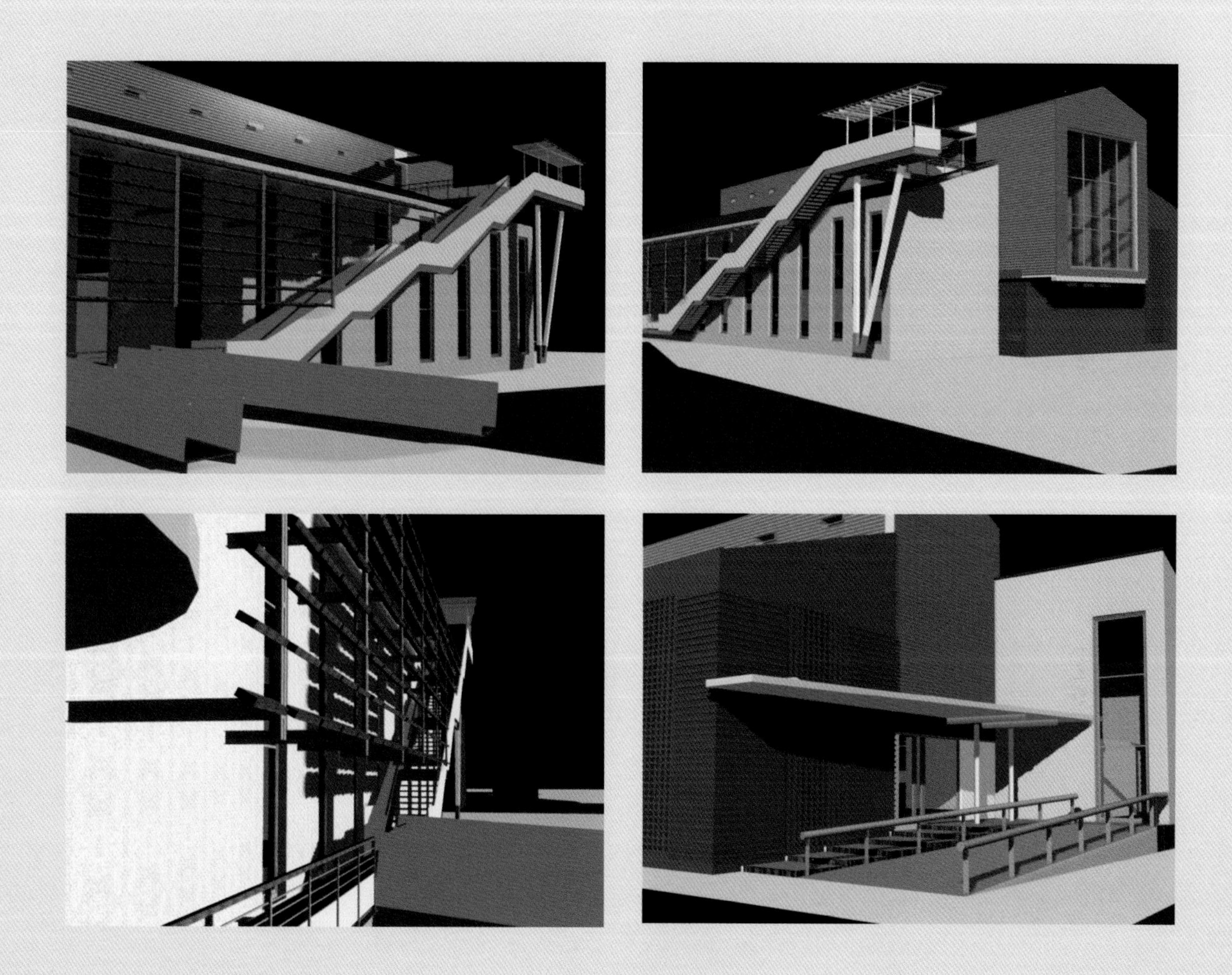

South and north elevations

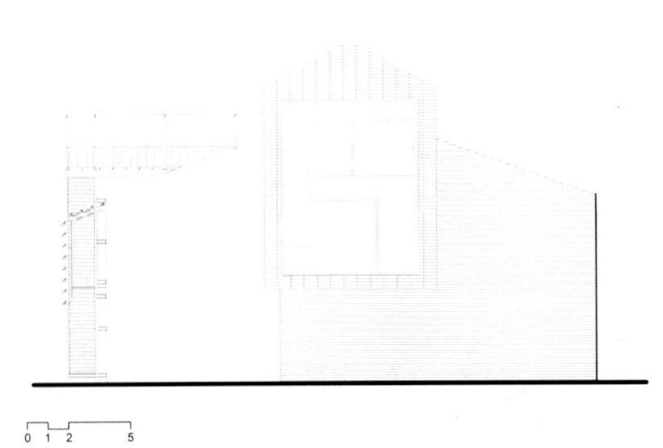

Cross sections

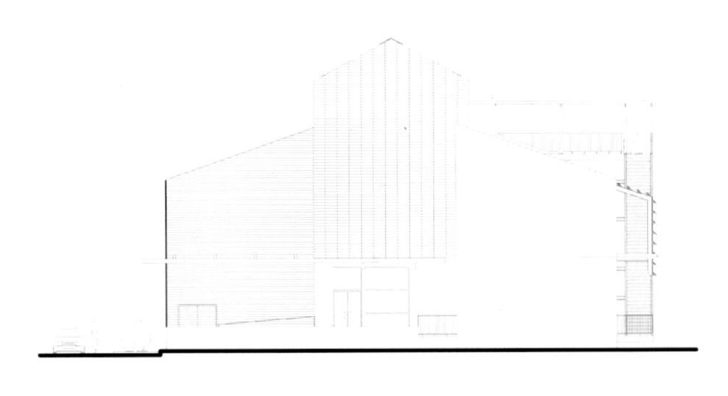

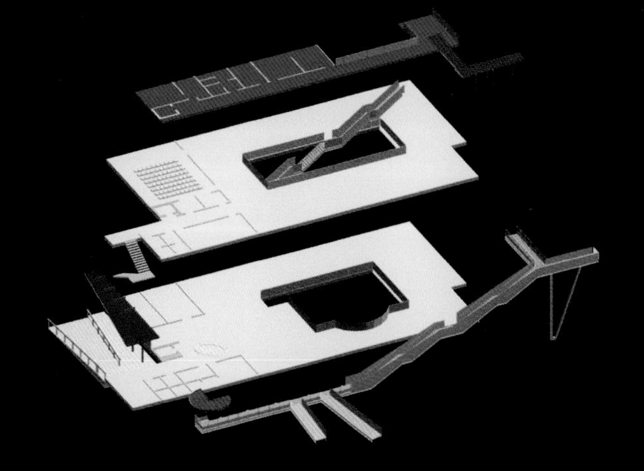

0 1 2 5

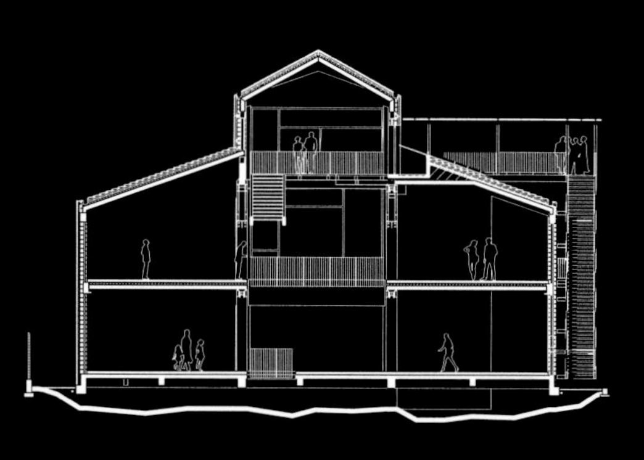

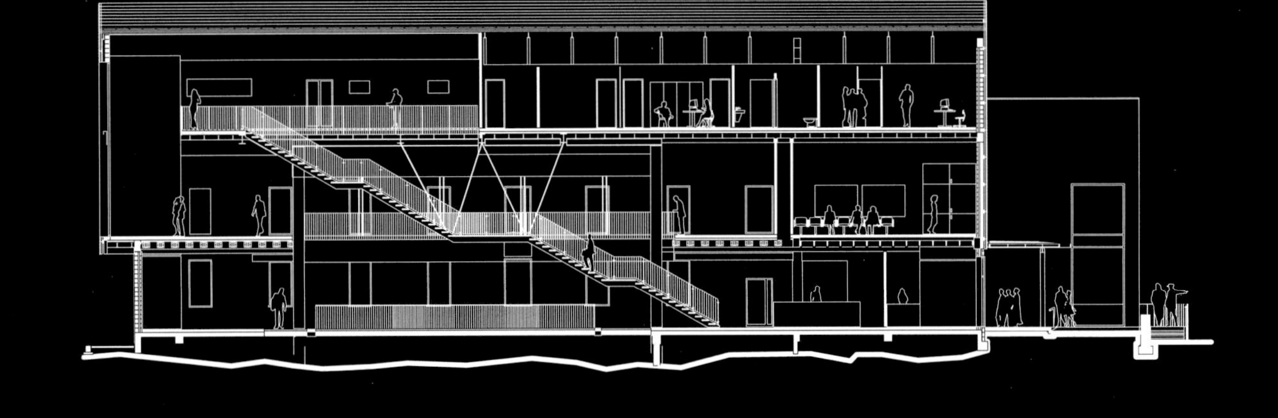
0 1 2 5

New university campus in the former Bligny Barracks, Savona

SPES scpa
Genoa University
Schedule: university campus
and advanced training centre
Period: 1997–2002, built in three
phases

'An existing site to be improved is considered the potential and economic energy of a project that must engage with the "figurative" schedule. One of the premises that underlies the strategy (which later becomes the method in nearly all projects) is "stratification". In this case, stratification was represented by the addition of a *brise-soleil* roof and a flooring system that sandwiches the existing structures; inclusion of the latter in turn defined how the levels of the ground, the horizon and the sky were to be treated. Virtual reorganisation of the industrial sheds has tended to dematerialise their compact forms and give them a sense of openness and lightness.

This aspect is linked to another premise of the project: the "suspension" occasionally made possible by the stream of light that "lifts" the base. The "banded" sky creates an effect of "night and day" in which differences are highlighted and objects-subjects invert their roles. It is, in short, a design based on places and situations, a work that offers fragments of solutions like a wide-screen cinema that can show different scenes at the same time. The architecture of 5+1 and Chaix and Morel has much in common with films, clips, focusing, references, the blurring of images (the "night" effect) and with the dynamic perceptions gathered from car windows that are liberated from their obscure regional associations; like its simple technologies, the design is manifest and radiant even at first inspection.

The project seems both strategic and playful in manner, with areas that are simple, easily understood and pleasant to experience but which are, above all, sequences, like the score of a piece of music ... or camera shots that bring into play the complexity of relationships. Essentially, these areas generate a chain reaction while exploring the "weft" of sensations and transparencies in which the project finds its rhythm'.

Brunetto De Batté

Model of the overall project

The media library

The Barracks
before the works

Plan of the first
three phases

Transformation

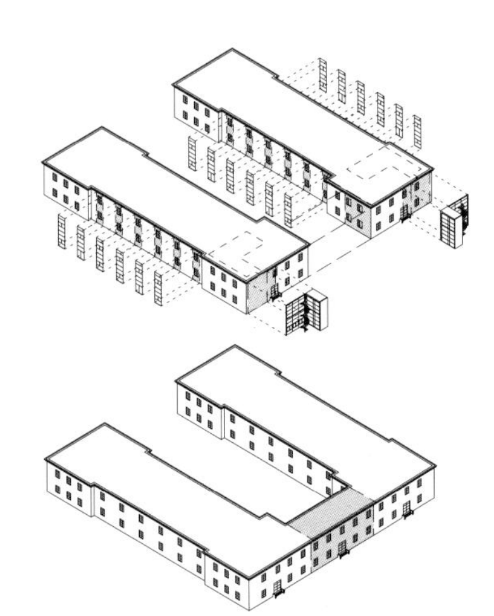

The two systems:
soil/wood

The aim of the project was to create a functional, spatial and psychological transformation of a set of military education buildings into a complex that represents:

- a real and symbolic opportunity for the local community: a training area must interact actively with both the cultural world of the private citizen and the business world;

- exploitation of the natural features of the place in relation to its new function: wide windows protected by the same type of *brise-soleil* roof that covers all the campus buildings let the natural world enter what were uncommunicative buildings transforming them into places of activity and exchange;

- exploitation of open spaces: a university campus and training site is also a place of creativity and surprises; careful planning of the open spaces between the buildings for particular purposes (sport, relaxation, open air performances, social exchange) was a complementary element of the project and of equal importance to the buildings.

The two systems:
sky/fibrocement

The west buildings

Plan

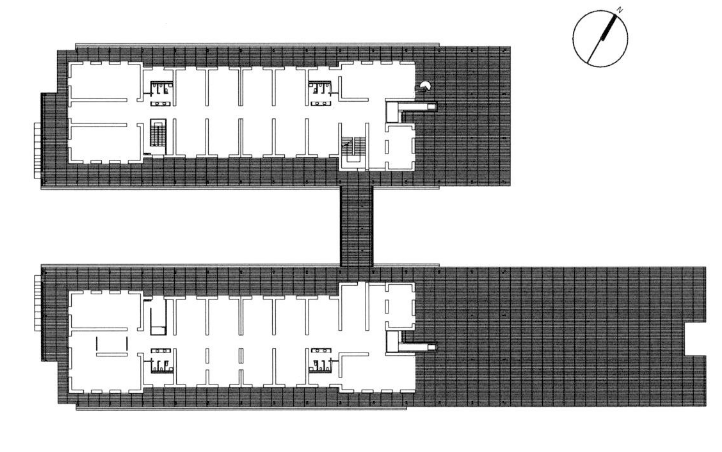

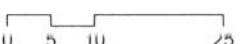

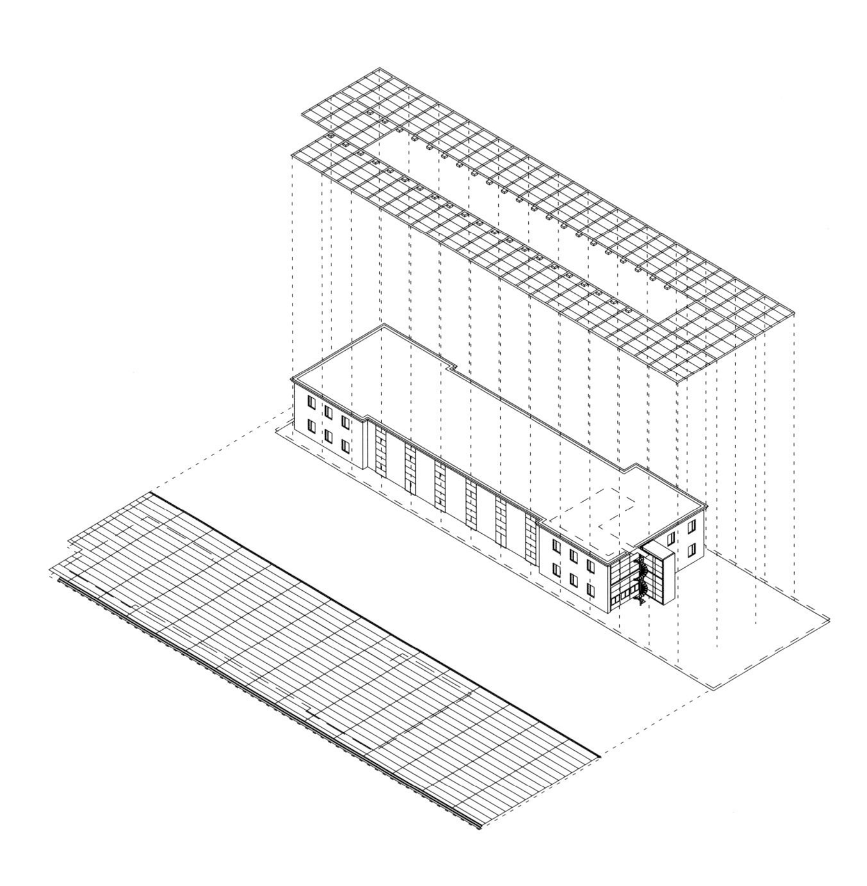

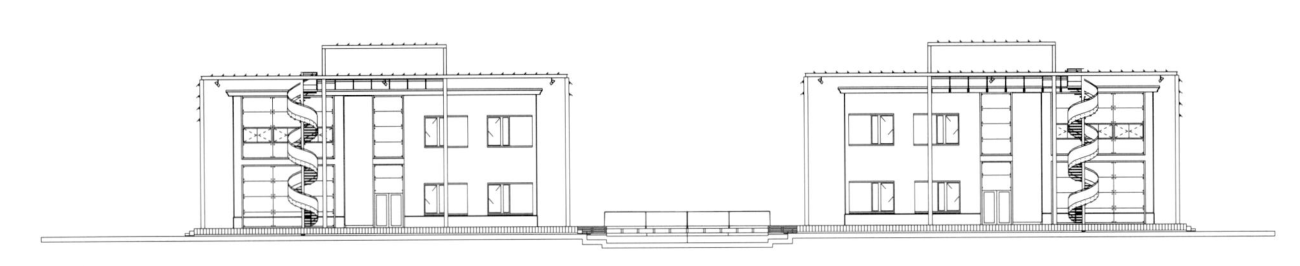

West elevation

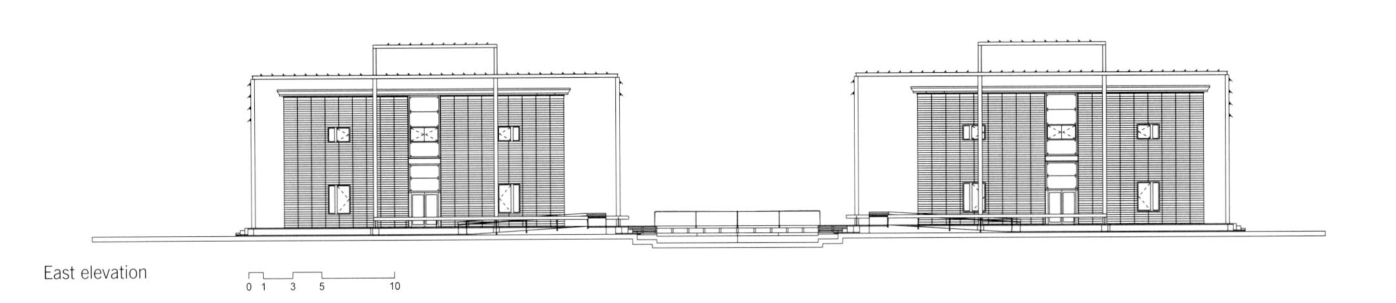

East elevation

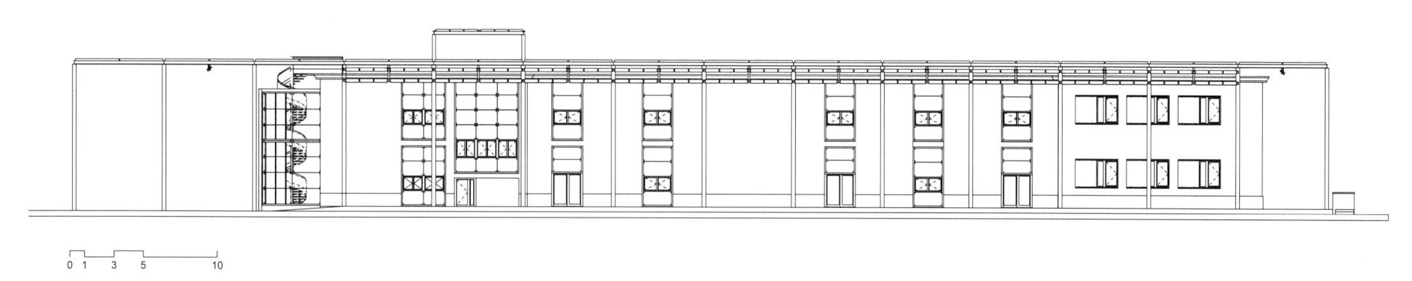

North elevation

Longitudinal section

Cross sections

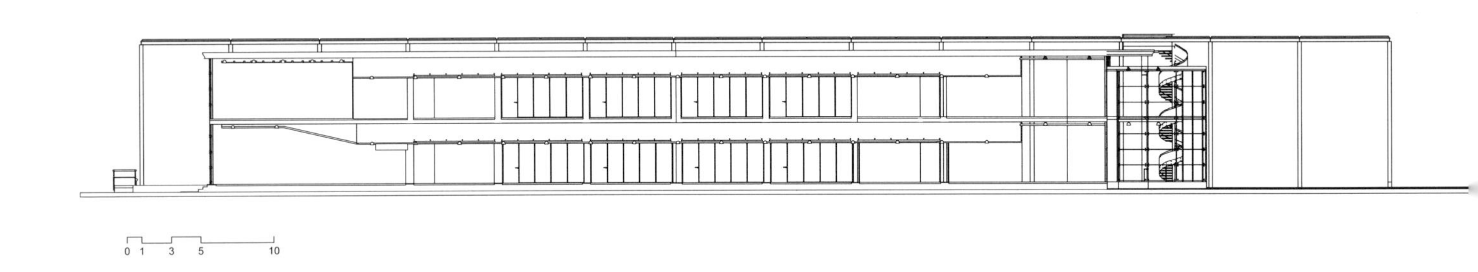

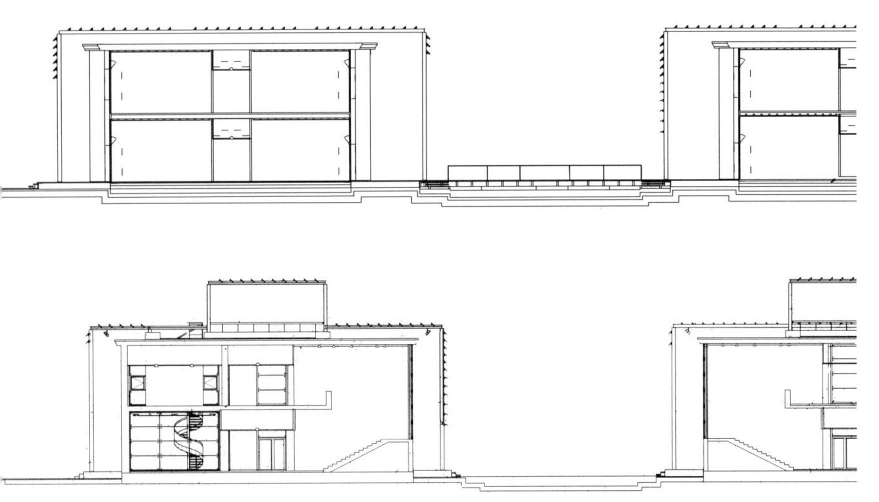

The media library

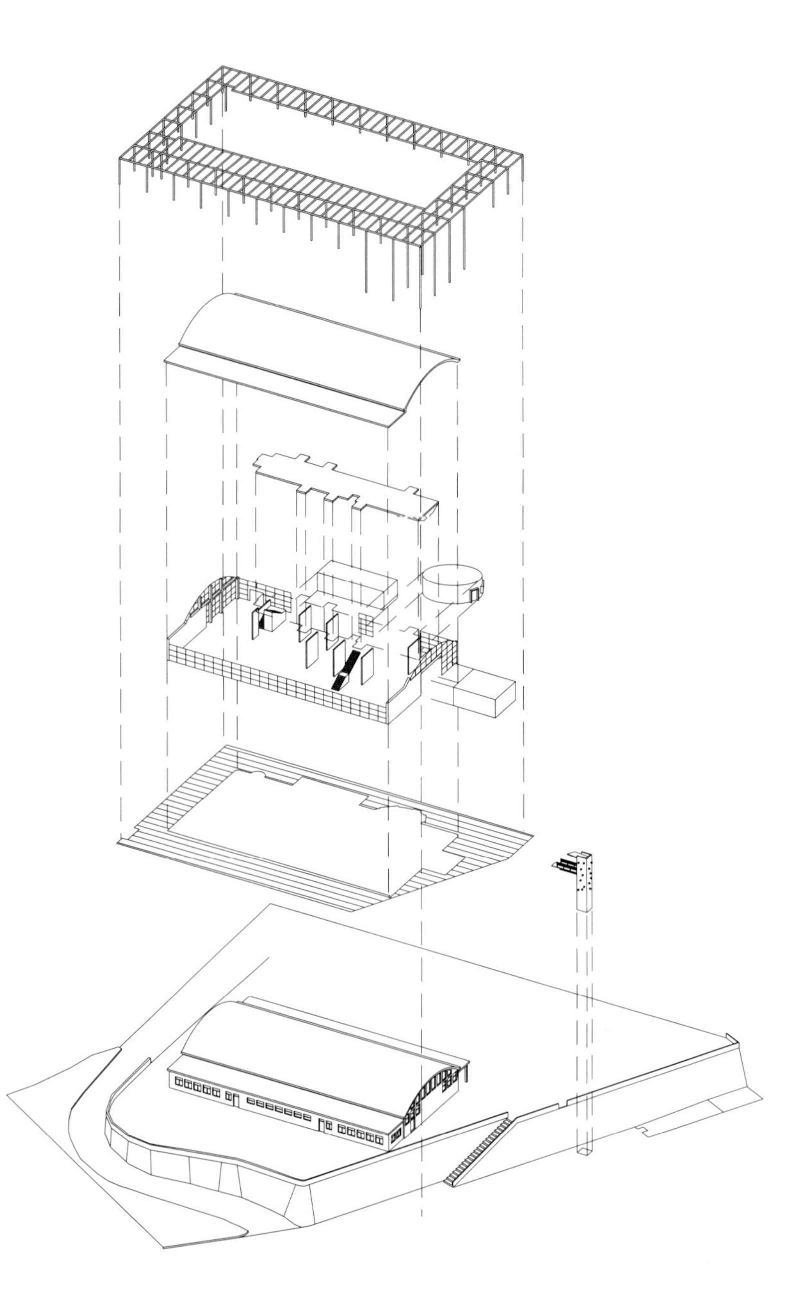

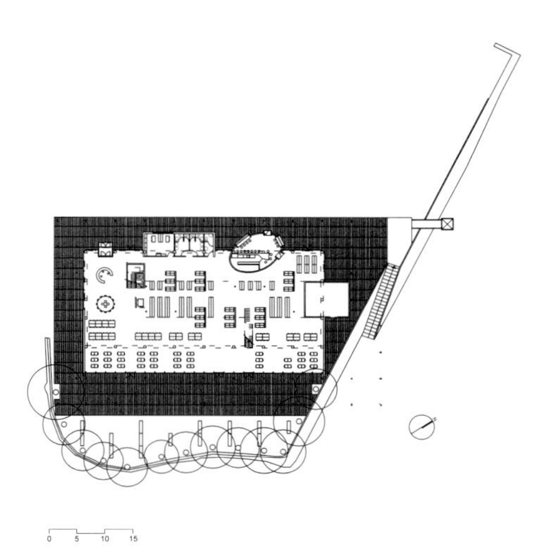

West elevation

0 1 3 5 10

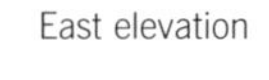
East elevation

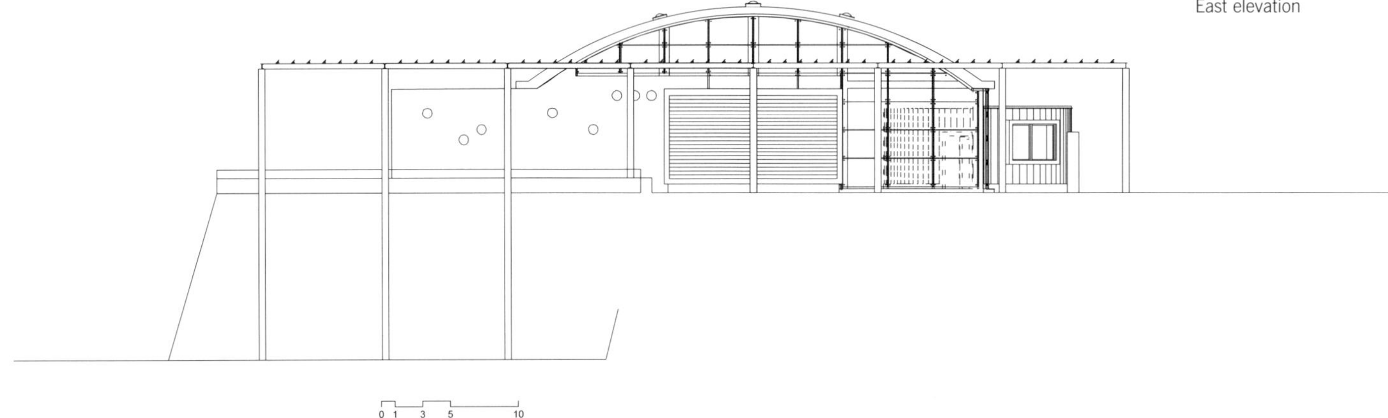

The egg-bar

The reading room

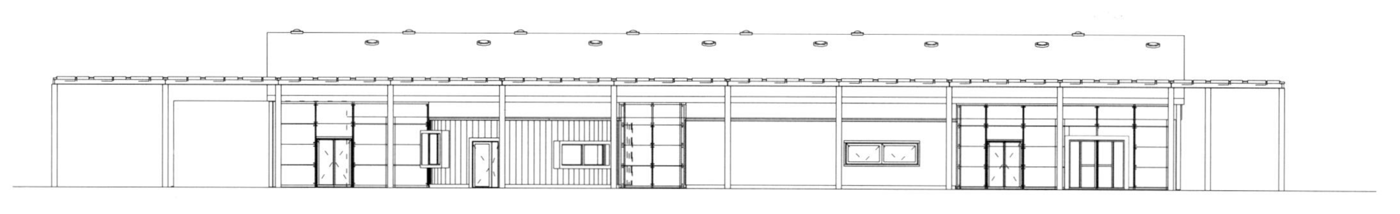

North elevation

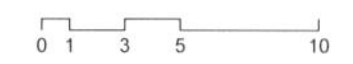

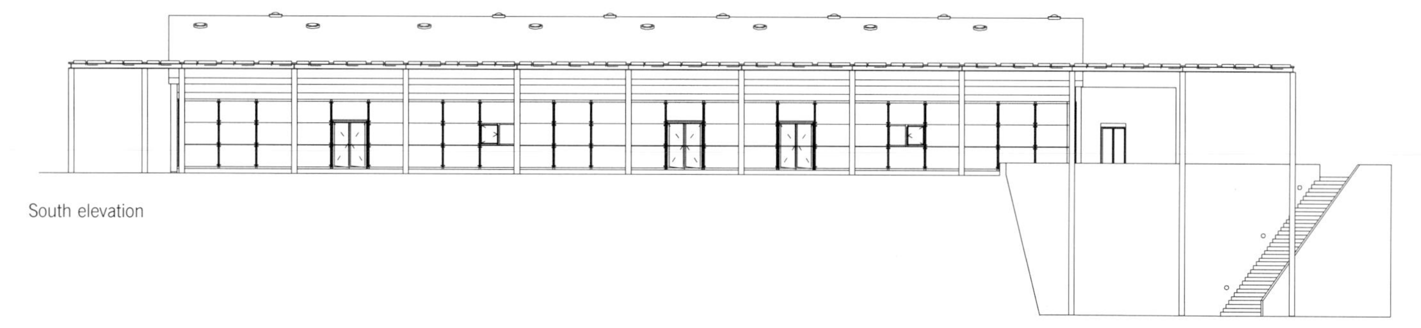

South elevation

Internal views

Longitudinal section

Cross section

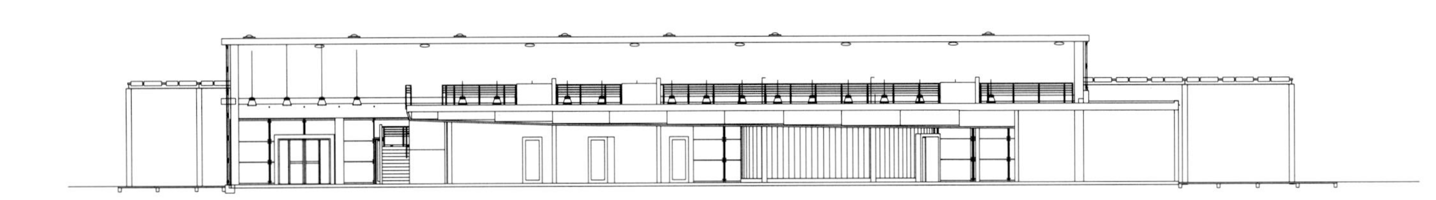

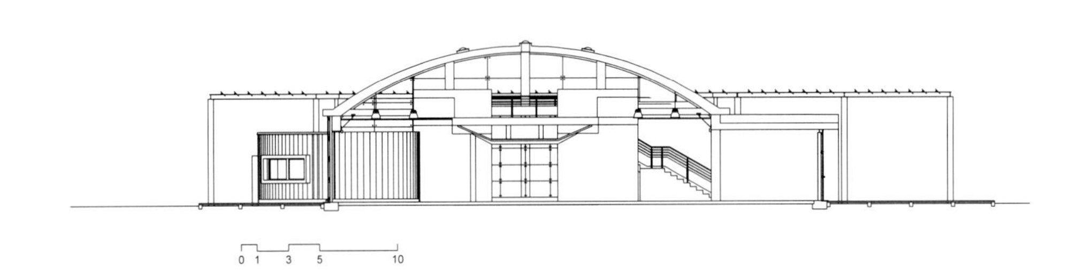

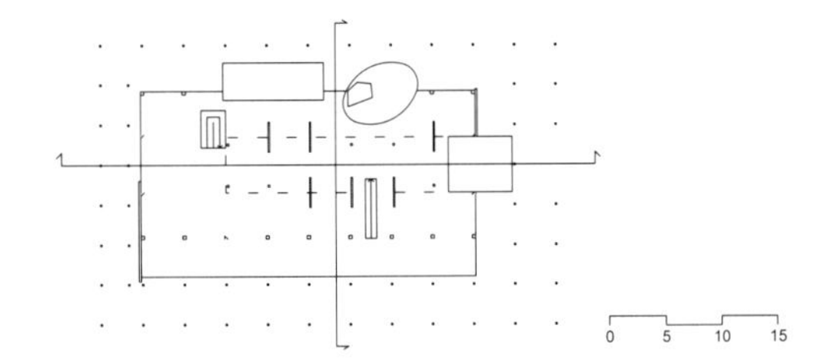

It's better not to understand

It's really better not to understand or to understand poorly or to misunderstand: it's only at this point that discussion can begin. It's only at that moment that the brain begins to operate. The spark of intuition, the flash of experience, and the cascade of images consolidate and take shape when matched with dimensions, functions and technology.
It would be wonderful to know where a fragile, initial flicker of intuition came from and how it almost 'magically' gets transformed into the schedule. Metamorphosis is slow and often contradicts itself along the way. The heights of initial passion are slowly strengthened by emotional foundations. We search for ideas that already exist, waiting to be transformed into reality. These ideas have materialised through a variety of styles and terms and are ready to be examined in depth and developed.

Sebastiano Brandolini

What our cities are longing for

It is impossible to be an architect and not comment on the state of our cities. The streets, restaurants and shops have become the main sites of social interaction and there are increasingly few places that bring people of different age, race and economic status together, and which, in addition, represent their collective function architecturally. Historians speak of squares and public buildings in the Middle Ages, of churches during the Counter-Reformation, of railway stations and department stores during the nineteenth century, and of factories and offices in the twentieth, but the question of what architects can and ought to do today is ever more pressing if they wish to give a recognisable three-dimensional form to the messy city layouts of the twenty-first century. Low-cost shoe outlets and concrete blocks containing cinemas are not enough, nor are the huge shopping centres stretched along the highways. Since 1980, museums have been making a comeback as a public area but there must be a limit to what can be remembered and celebrated of our past.

These are worries that pervade the complex projects on which the dynamic 5+1 group has worked over the last few years. I have met them on several occasions — for work, pleasure and debate — in Milan and Genoa, both in chaotic city centres and the ugliness of the suburbs. More than once I did not know which of them would turn up and it was always a surprise in the end. Their projects are never signed individually but only as a group. Each project has the mission of creating something and of enriching its context, whether in form, materials or agenda, by highlighting the differences and contrasts of the place and, in the end, a clear, legible form will emerge, a well-defined form made of layers and overlaps. They do not strive after elegance or an archetype because 5+1 accept ugliness and incongruency; it is the architect's task to organise negative values and to hone reality but without going too far and ending up with negative results. If a city is to work with full efficiency, it must be able to embrace what is ugly and unwanted.

The relationship between a project and its surrounding environment must be respected because the image of a city can only be changed by degrees. The project for a leisure centre in San Donato Milanese condenses the idea that a city can be recreated and compressed into a single building. In this project, an industrial shed was transformed into an elegant multi-sided box that people could enjoy whether they arrived on foot or by car, from the city or from the nearby countryside. It is a quietly technological object that does not flaunt a controversial image. Its goals include a range of activities, some of which are visible, others not, and the result is that it is considered recreational but serious, i.e. a real public building for everyone.

Today we are attracted more by the various activities that a city offers than by the city itself. For too many architects, the city has become a cartoon. Like the camera of David Hockney or Gerhard Richter, 5+1 capture fragments of daily experience. In what is a sign of a collective mini-neurosis, they constantly observe their surroundings. Meanwhile, cities are all in search of their identities like hunters after their prey. For better or for worse, public spaces — whether internal, external or a mixture of both — form the notch of many of 5+1's projects: the promenades in Liguria, the new colonnades in the former Bligny Barracks in Savona, and the bridge and the gallery in San Donato Milanese are all projects that console and allow us to hope, because they reconcile the unavoidable physical characteristics of certain places with the legitimate aspirations of the city residents.

Leisure centre, San Donato Milanese

Plant spa
Milano Centrale spa
Schedule: Leisure centre
Surface area: 19,000 sqm
Period: 1999

The Leisure centre is to be part of a new district that might be defined as an Integrated Urban Park with specific characteristics and potentiality: it is a district that is mostly for pedestrian use but which can be easily accessed by cars, and which will be home to different 'functions'.

The transformation of the former AGL into an Leisure centre will retain much of the building's vertical and horizontal structures. The building will be mostly relined with a new facade of wooden screens and the line of the ground at the base will be redesigned.

New entrances will be created in the existing volume, the first will open onto the overhead walkway that crosses the roundabout and joins the church square, the second that connects to the residential area to the south, over the viaduct. The overhead walkway is of special importance to the whole project because of its visibility and its design qualities.

The facade will be transformed by removal of parts of it and silhouetting.

The Leisure centre will be mainly a place where various central functions of the city are carried out so the most numerous users will be local (residents of San Donato Milanese). Consequently, the project not only offers entertainment but architectural features such as the way in which the external spaces converge to become internal spaces and the fact that the routes are natural and fluid. The volume of the existing building is divided into three functionally distinct and adjacent parts that connect horizontally and vertically.

San Donato Milanese

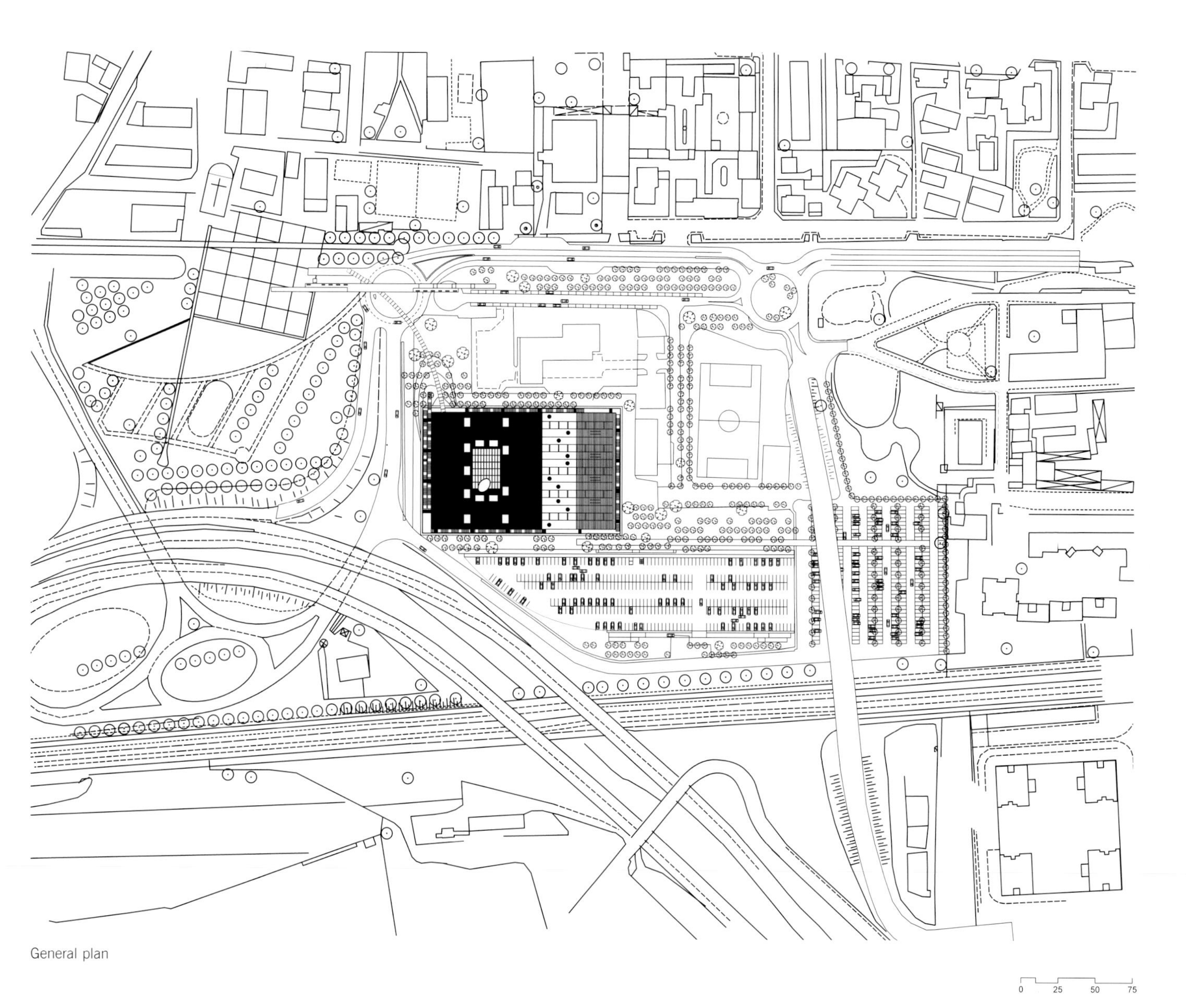

General plan

Ground floor plan

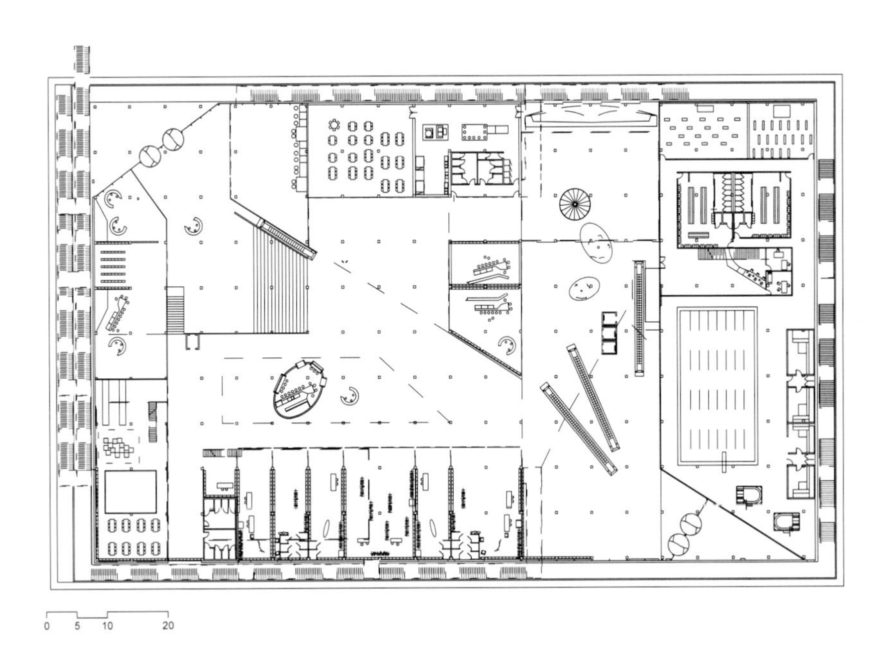

Main elevations

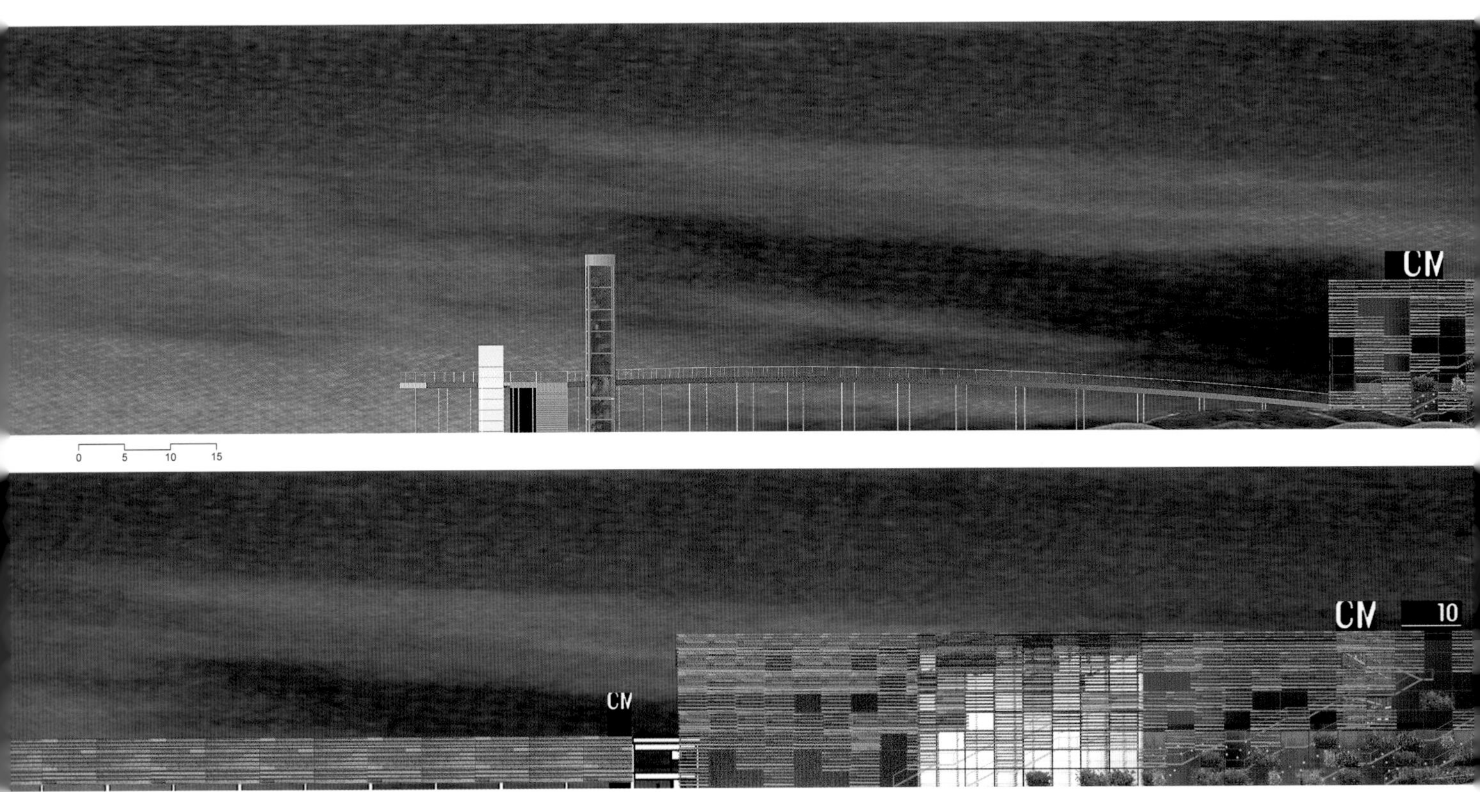

First floor plan

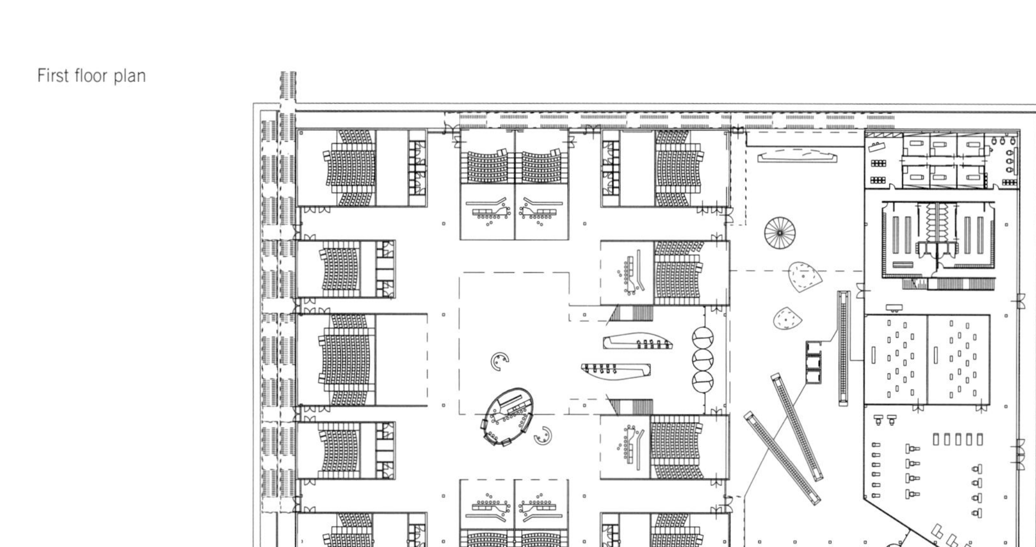

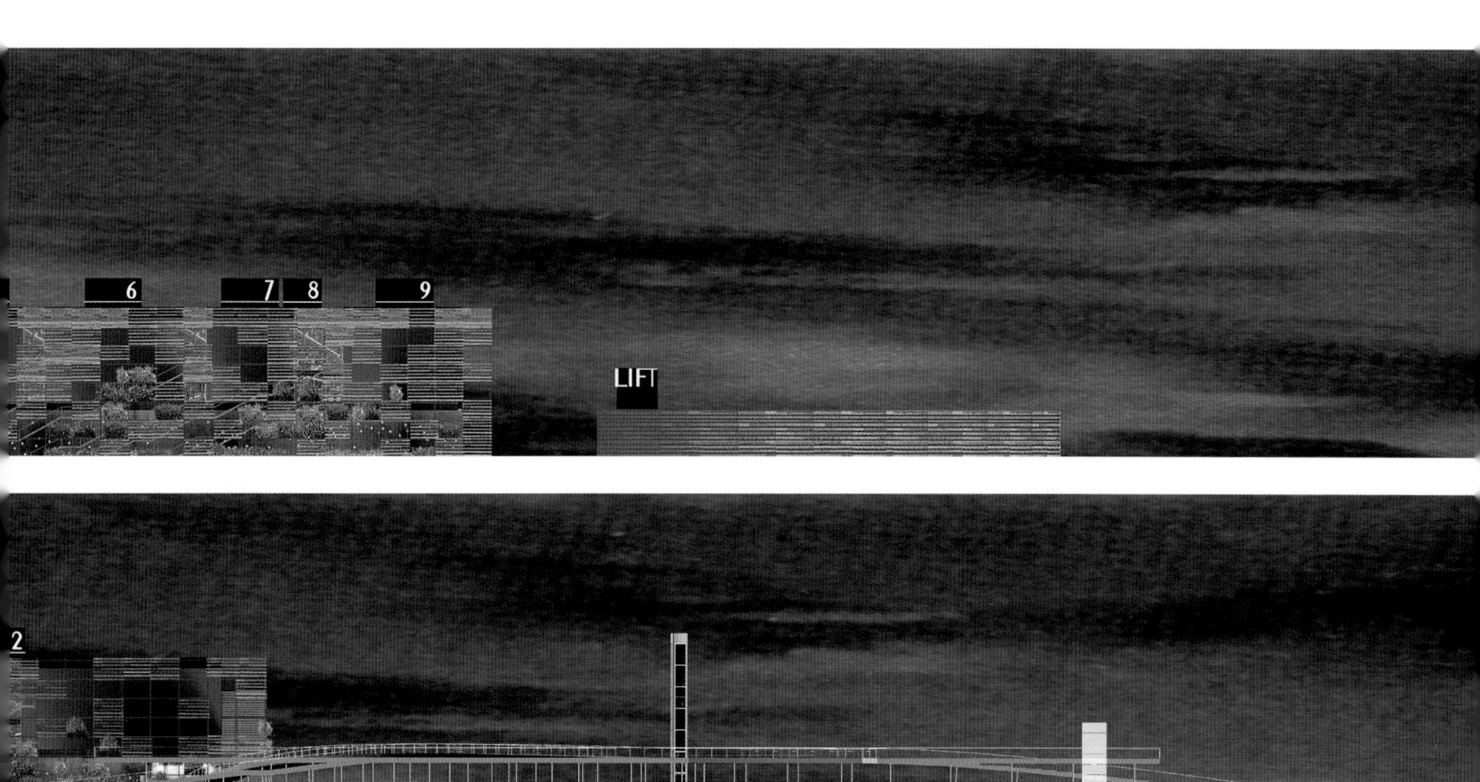

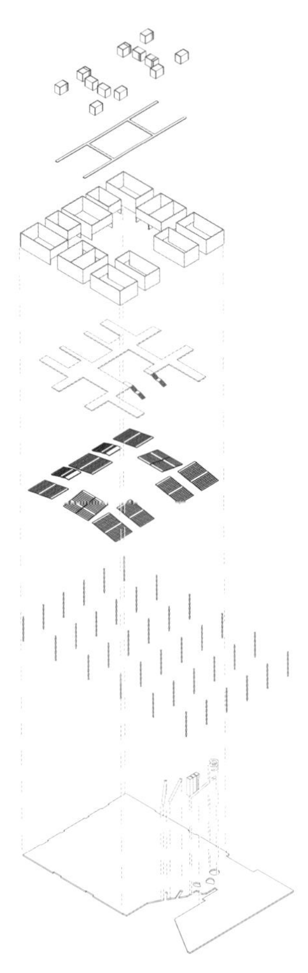

Longitudinal section

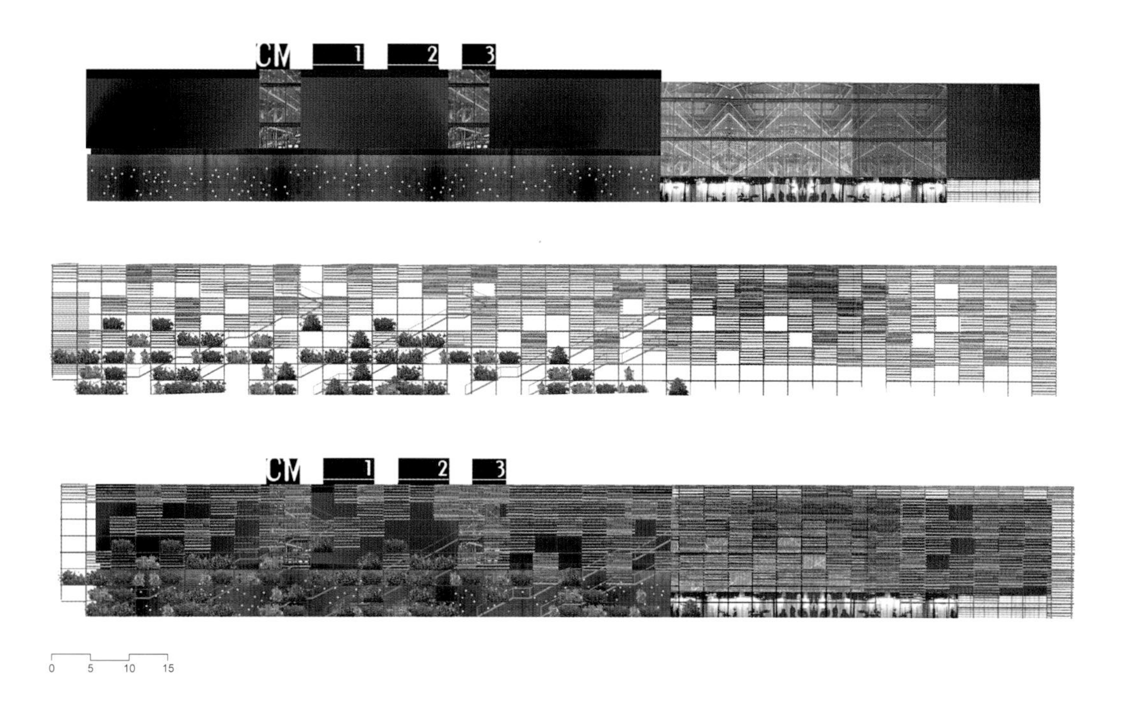
CM
1
2
3
CM
1
2
3
0
5
10
15

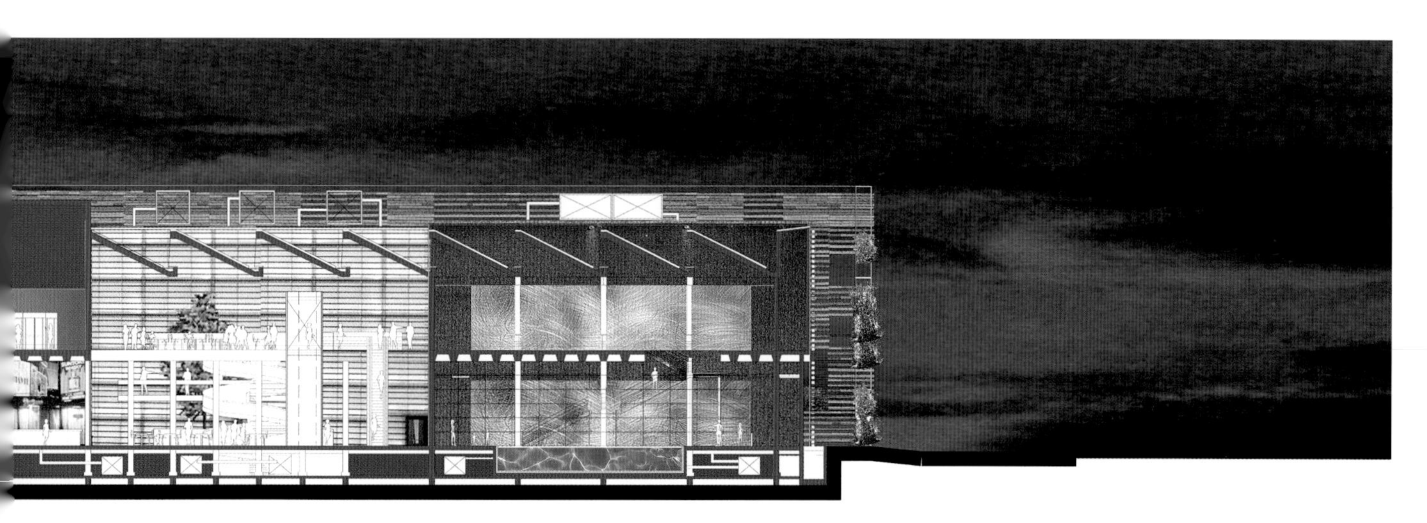

Longitudinal section

View of the ground floor foyer

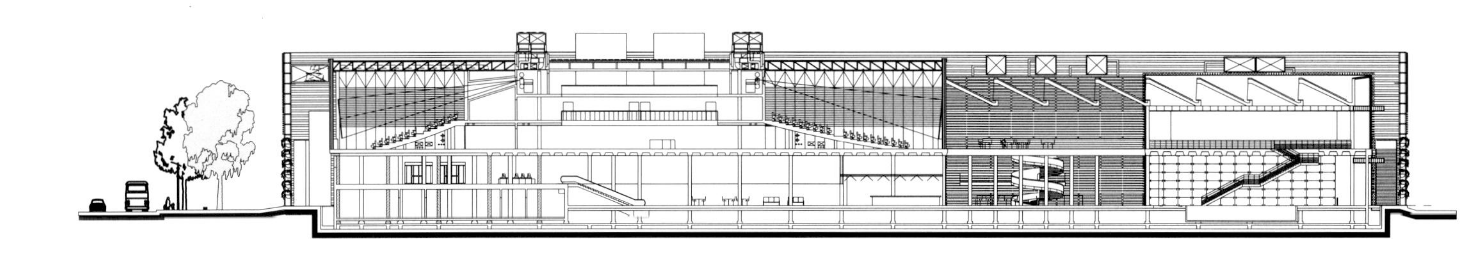

Cross section

View of the first
floor foyer

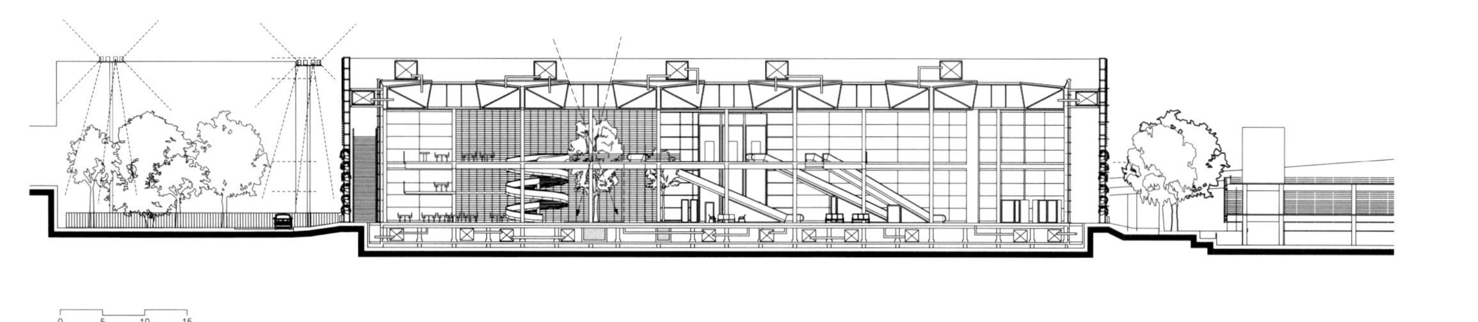

SDM

comune di san donato milanese

centro culturale espositivo
e dell'intrattenimento
nell'edificio ex-AGL

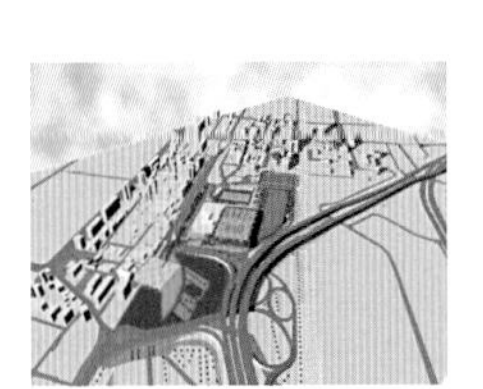
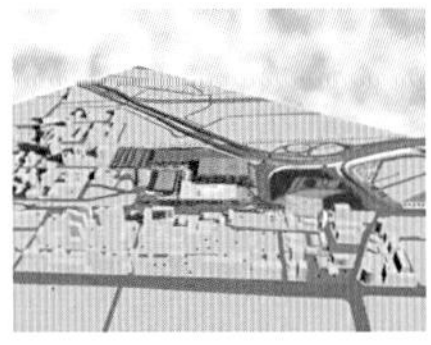

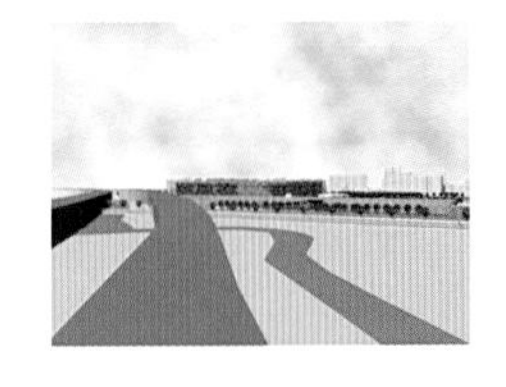

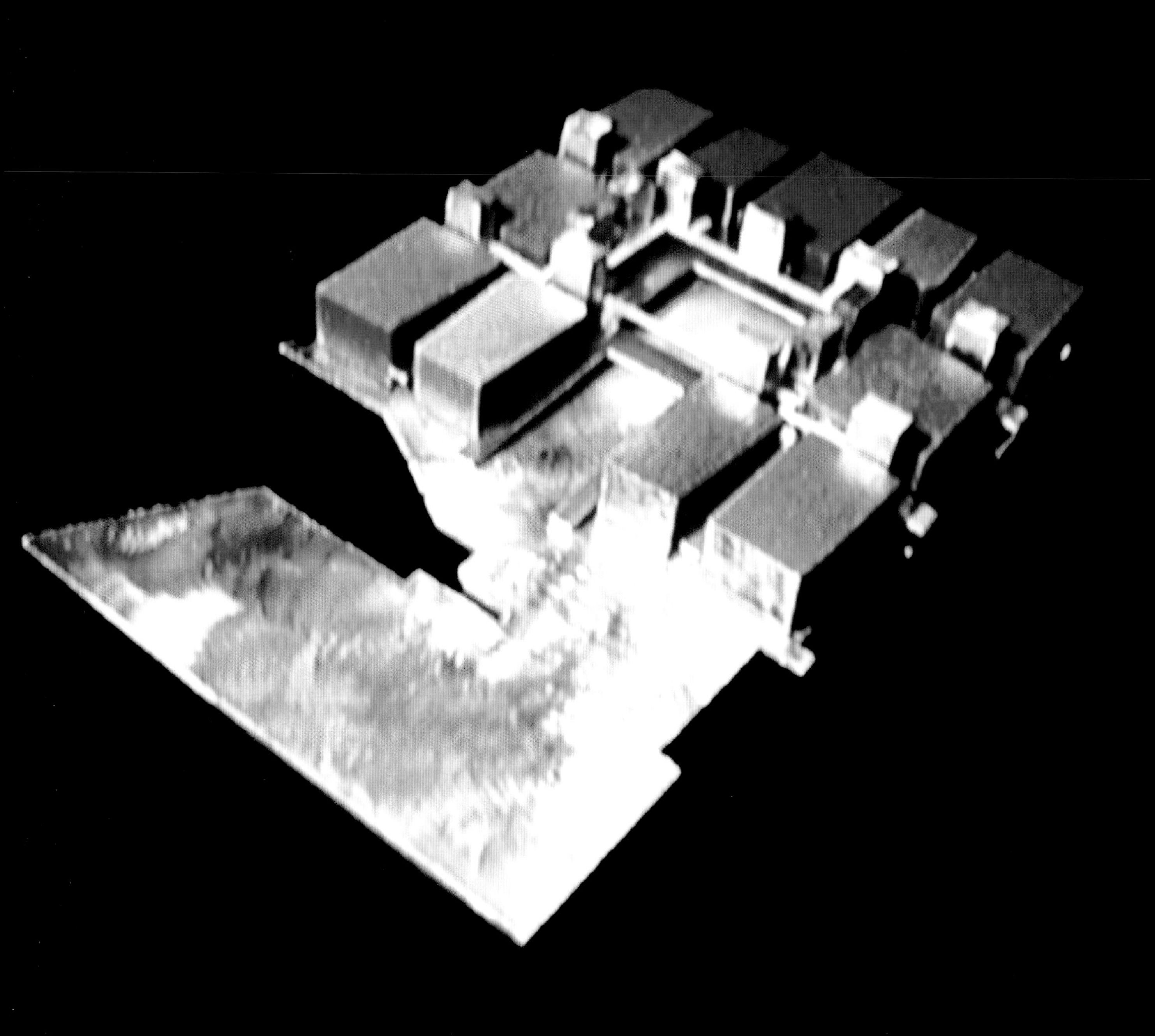

New hospital centre, Biella

ASL 12, Biella
Schedule: new hospital centre, 900 beds, psychiatric unit, auditorium (350 seats), operating block (12 theatres)
Surface area: 124,000 sqm
Cost: 270 billion lire
Period: project 1997–2000; works 2001–05

The technological and normative requirements for a new 900 bed hospital in Biella plain seem to have the power to suffocate any archaeological inspiration but the objectives of the architectural input and functional impositions took these forms:

- an evident spatial and compositional translation of the schedule: the building comprises three elements — a base that hosts all the work zones, the two sets of wards and five satellite areas (operating theatres, day hospital, conference centre, technical plants arca and a psychiatric unit building);
- the two floors are overlaid to create a sort of pedestal-base-plinth on which the two sets of wards lie along the main axis;
- buildings of various shapes and functions are attached to this central rectangle;
- the operating theatres are connected directly with the surgery wards;
- the diversity of the day hospital and outpatients' departments is underlined by their irregular shape and vertical design;
- the nucleus of the conference centre can be entered directly from the atrium so that even external groups can make use of it;
- the technical plants area stands separate in the south-east corner of the complex, only partly rising above ground level to reduce both visual impact and the noise level;

special carc was paid to thc psychological perception of the exterior of the complex from the point of view of the patients on the inside. The facade of the wards has been created in several skins that range from the transparency of the skin that adheres to the building to a set of wooden *brise-soleil* that gives shade from the sun but permits the patients to look out.

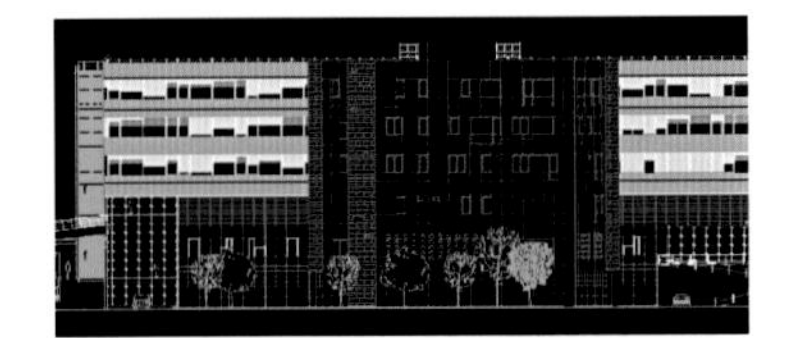

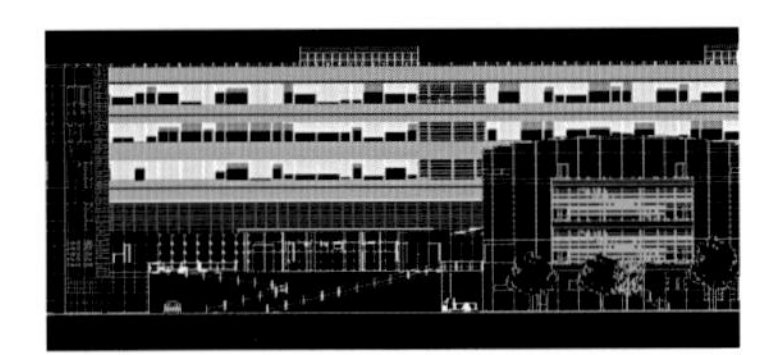

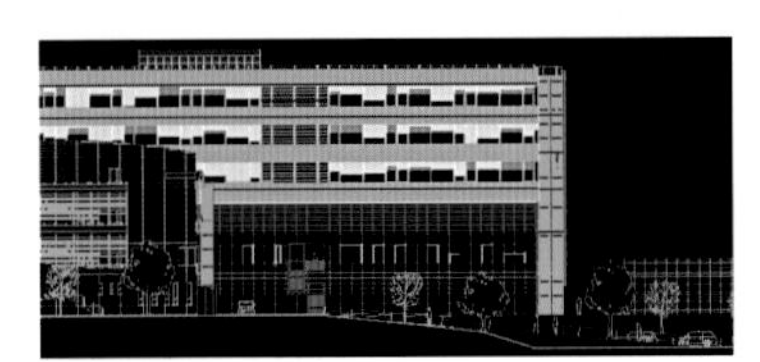

Project layout

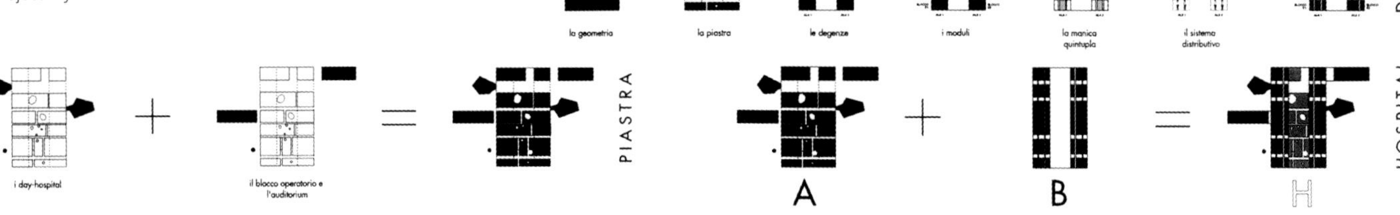

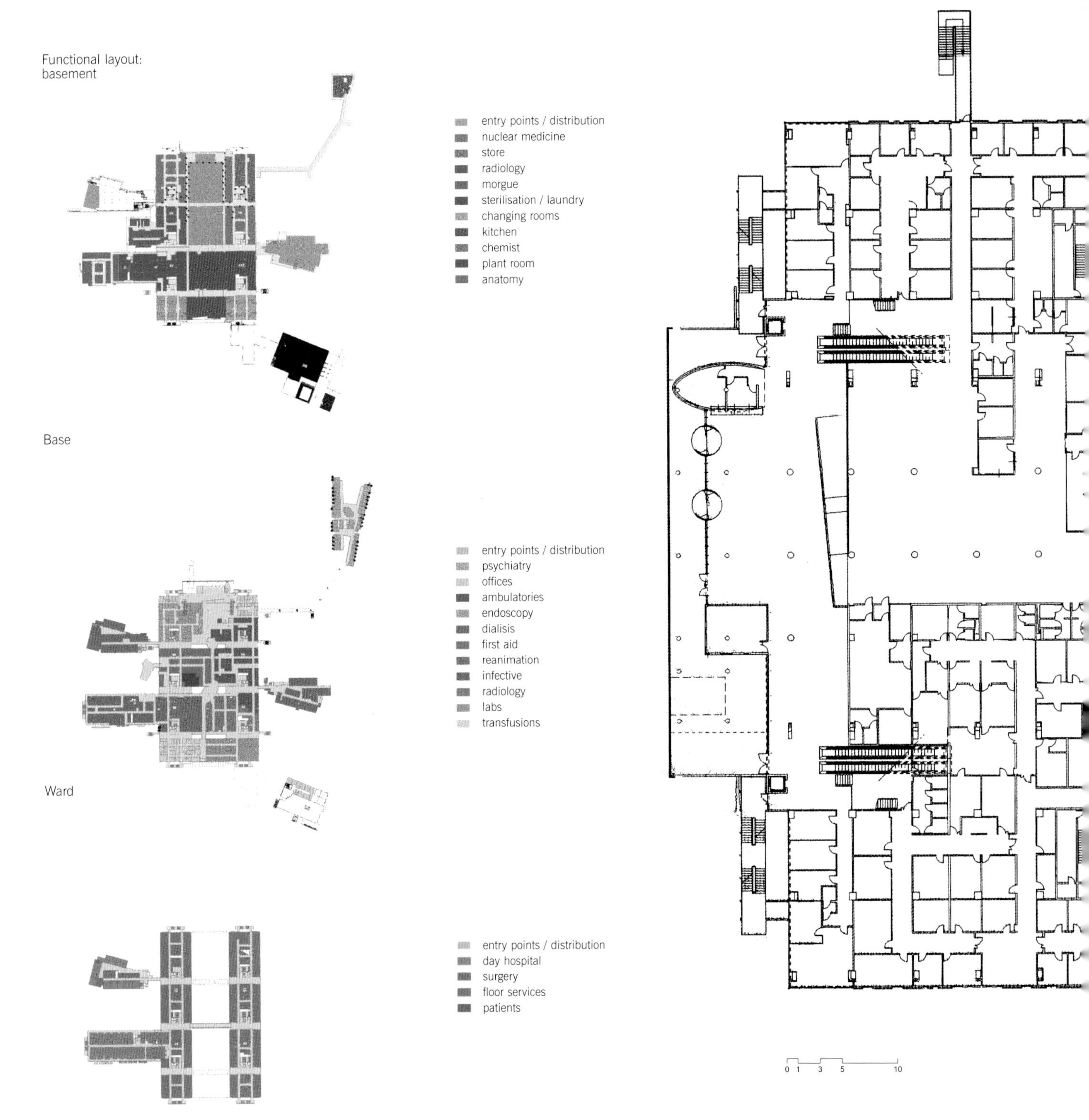
Functional layout:
basement
entry points / distribution
nuclear medicine
store
radiology
morgue
sterilisation / laundry
changing rooms
kitchen
chemist
plant room
anatomy
Base
entry points / distribution
psychiatry
offices
ambulatories
endoscopy
dialisis
first aid
reanimation
infective
radiology
labs
transfusions
Ward
entry points / distribution
day hospital
surgery
floor services
patients
0 1 3 5 10

Model of the psychiatric pavilion and auditorium

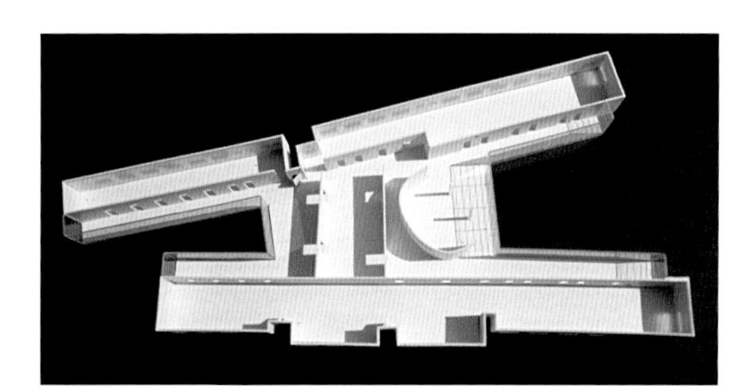

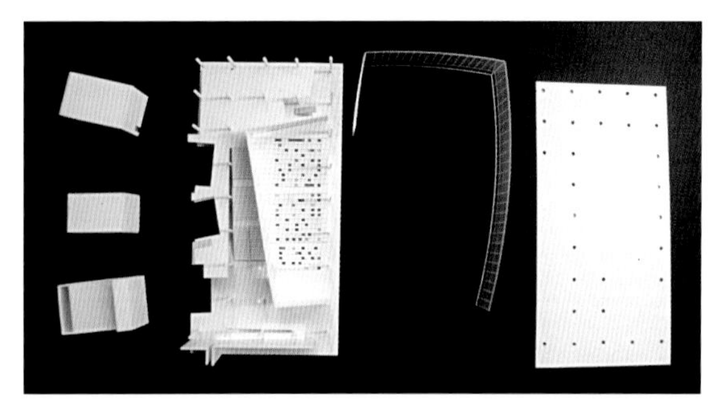

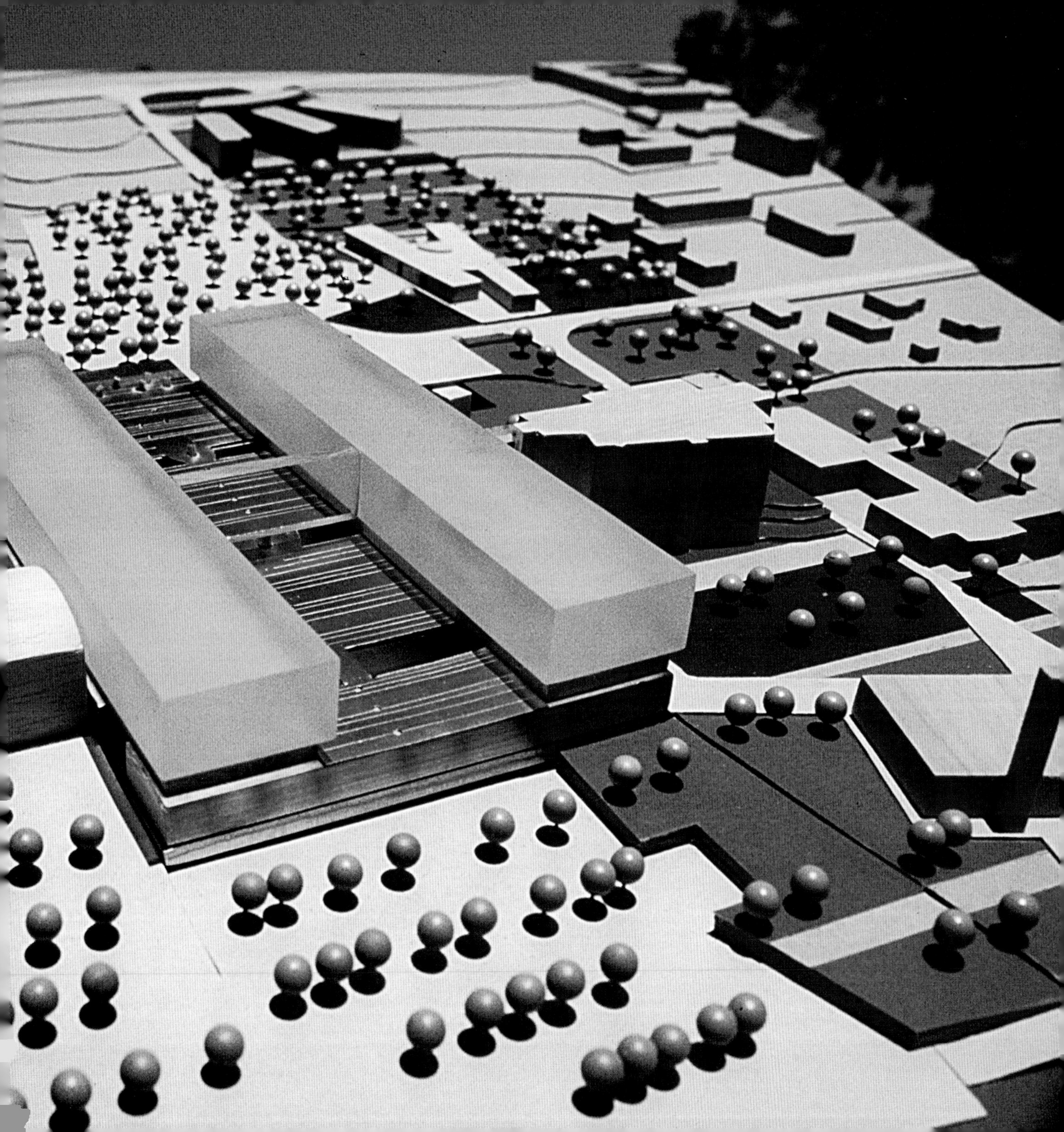

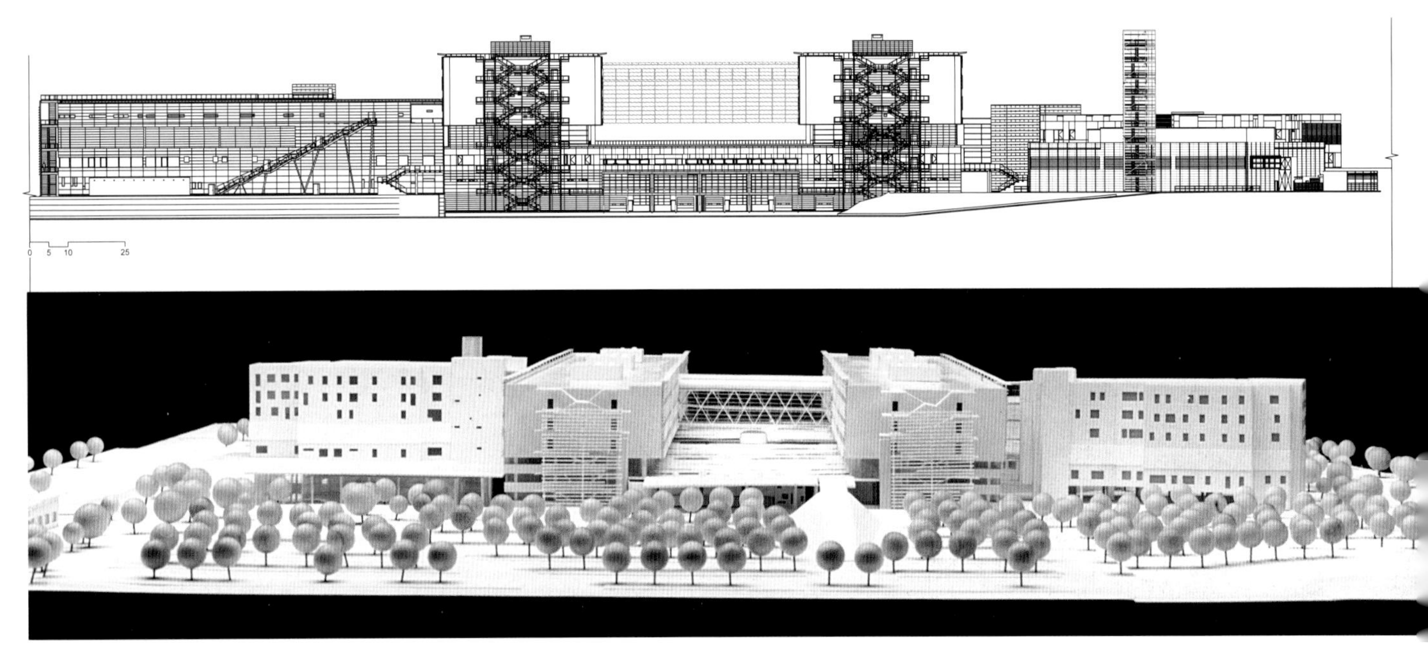

South elevation and view of the north face of the model

Next page: west elevation and view of the east face of the model

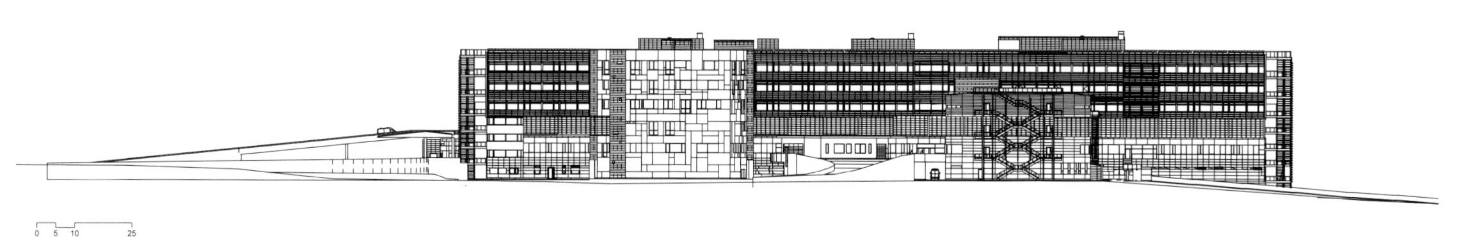
0 5 10 25

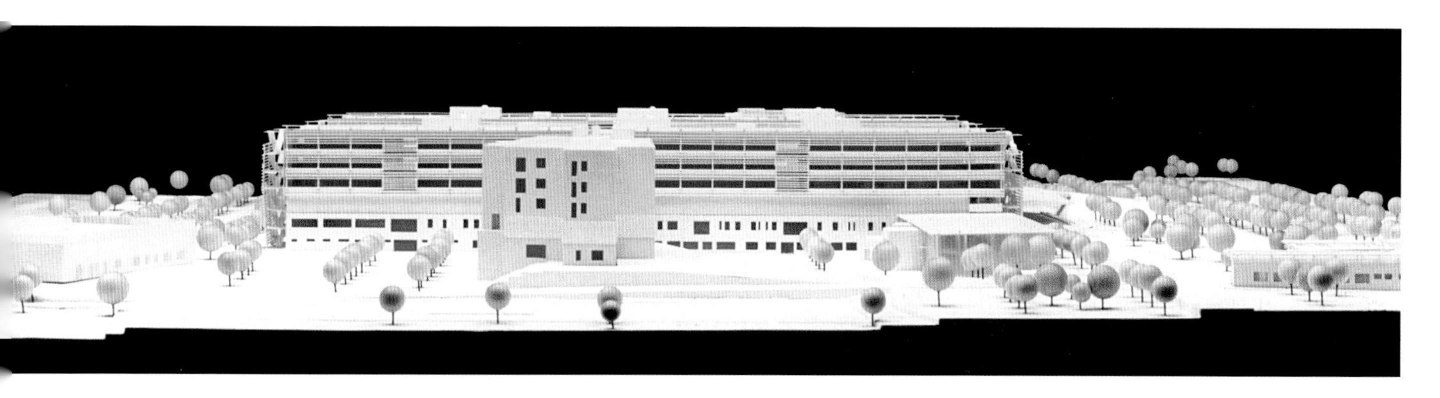

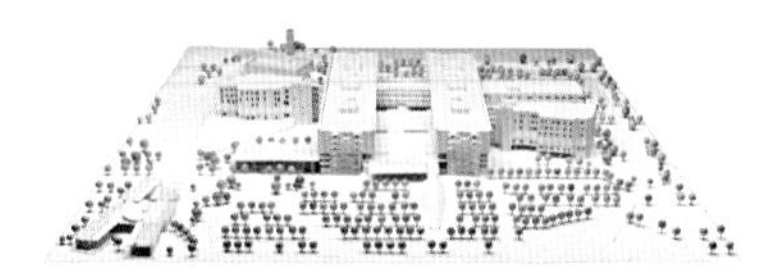

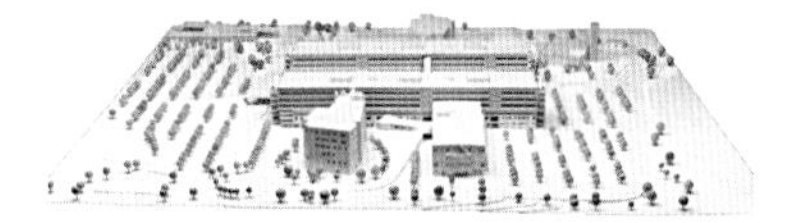

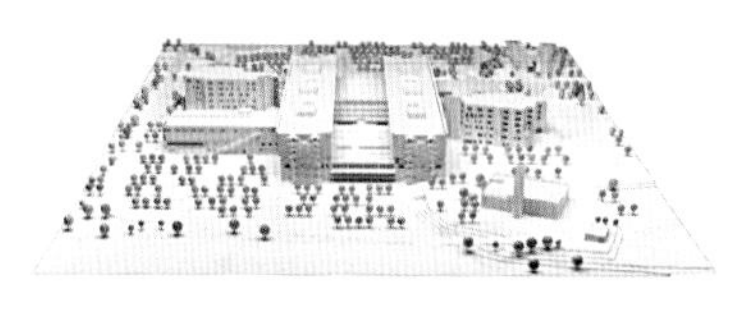

The wood facade system·
study images,
model and section/view
of the facade

Bottom: cross section
of the atrium

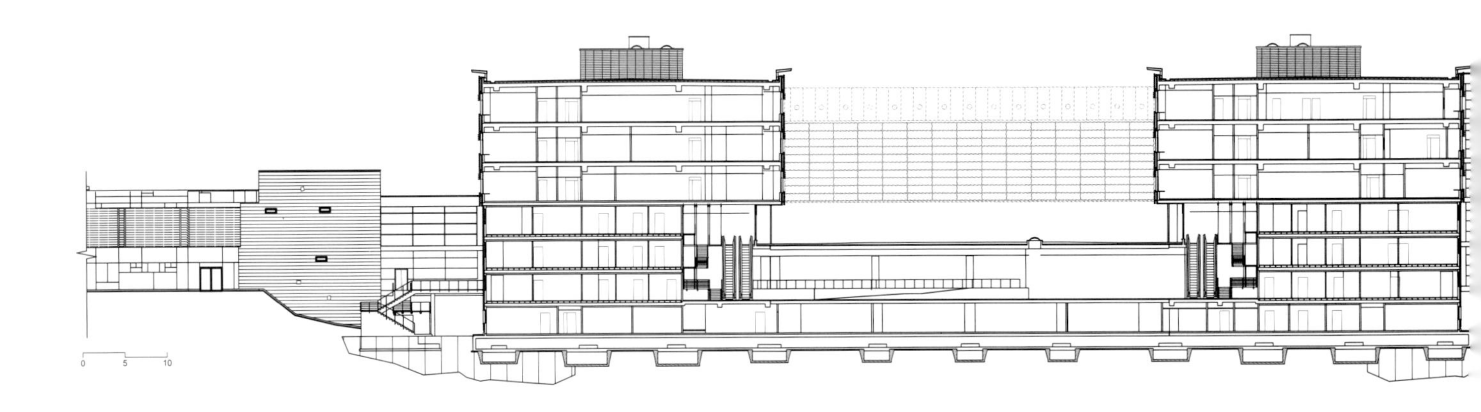

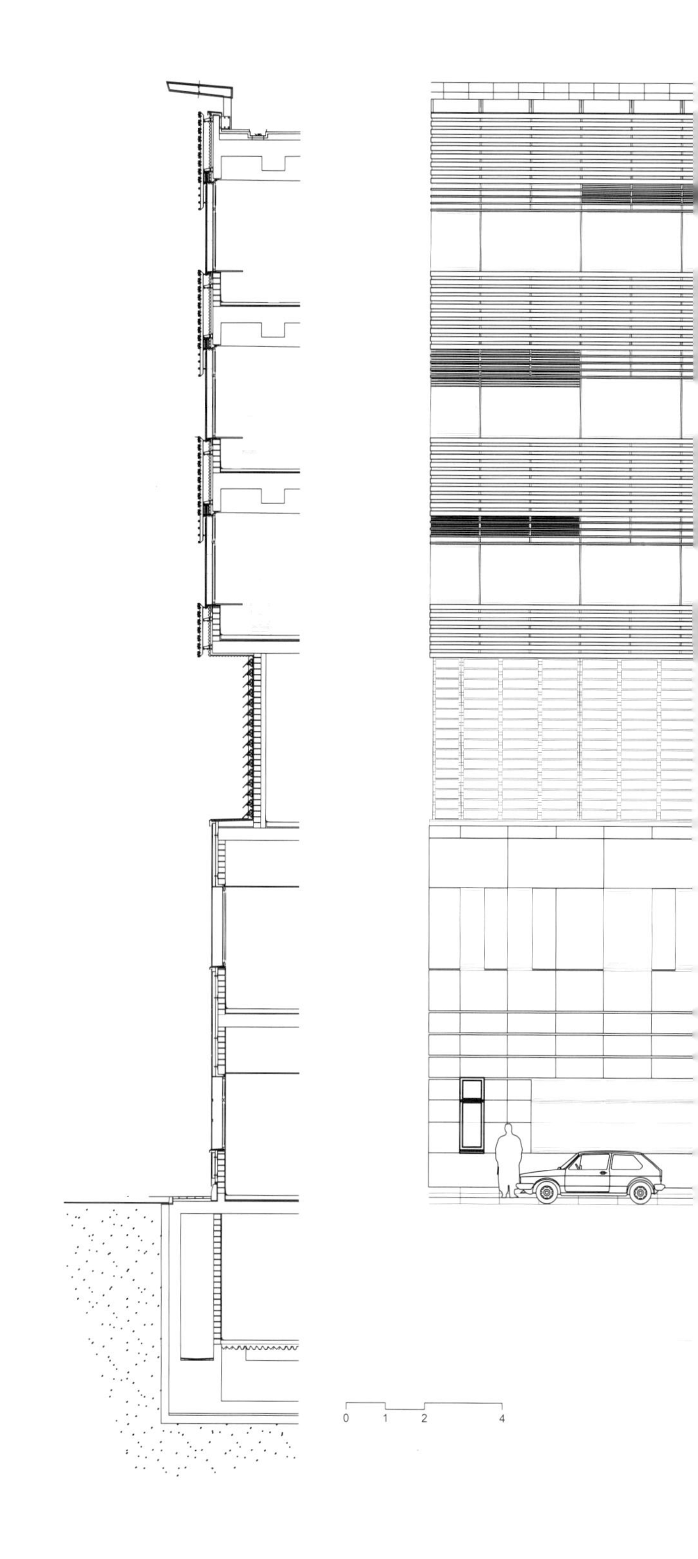
0
1
2
4

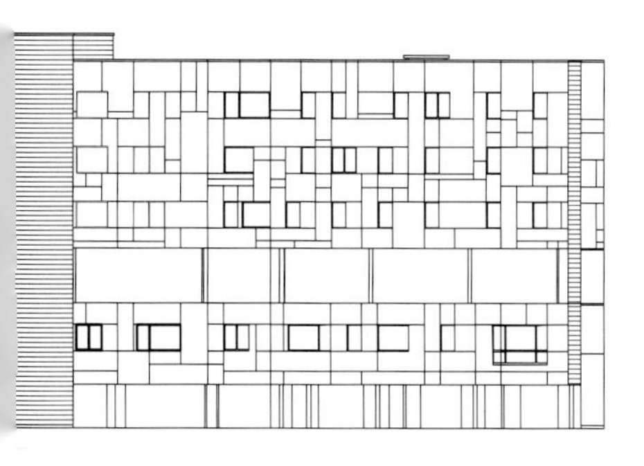

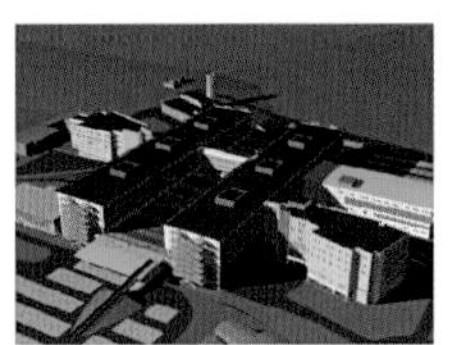
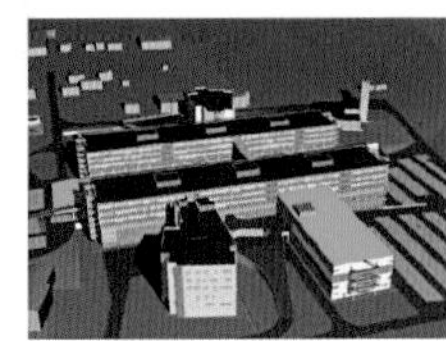

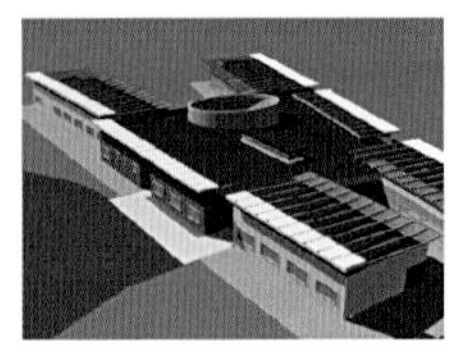

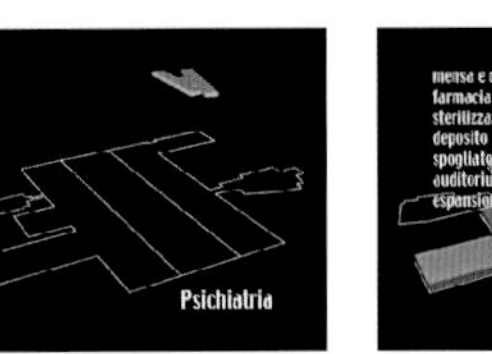
Psichiatria

mense e cucina
farmacia
sterilizzazione
deposito
spogliatoi
auditorium
espansioni future
Piano Seminterrato
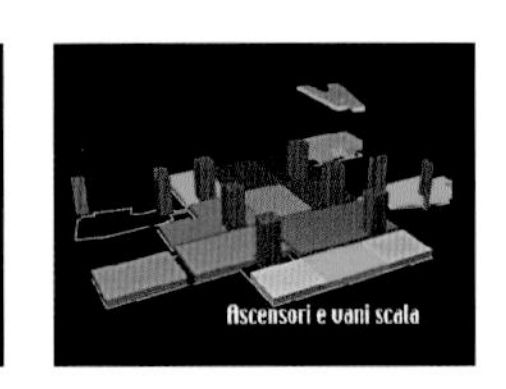
Ascensori e vani scala

ambulatori specialistici
dialisi
DEA
endoscopia
radiodiagnostica
rianimazione
Piano Terra
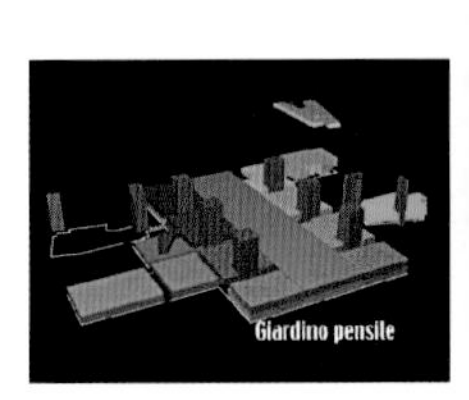
Giardino pensile

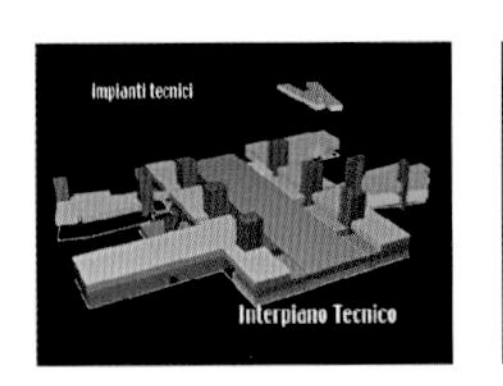
impianti tecnici
Interpiano Tecnico
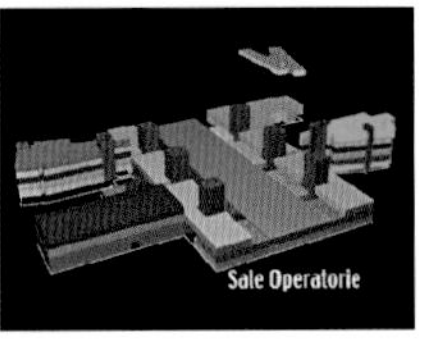
Sale Operatorie
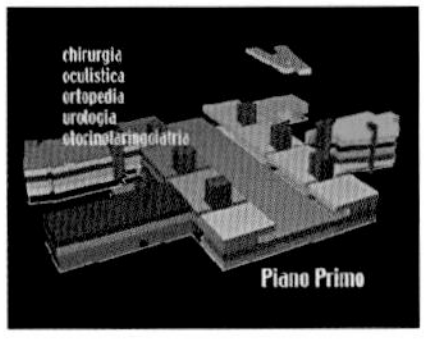
chirurgia
oculistica
ortopedia
urologia
otorinolaringoiatria
Piano Primo
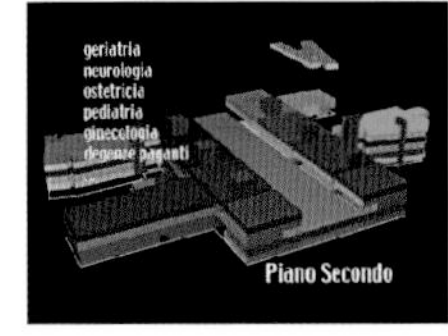
geriatria
neurologia
ostetricia
pediatria
ginecologia
degenze paganti
Piano Secondo
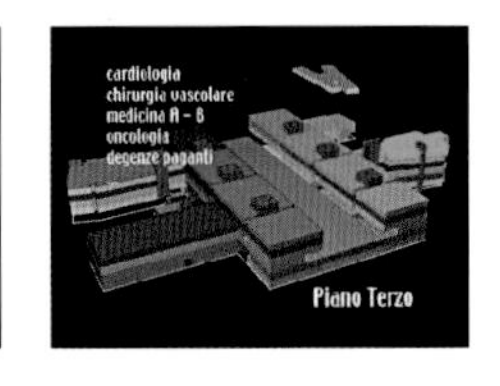
cardiologia
chirurgia vascolare
medicine A - B
oncologia
degenze paganti
Piano Terzo

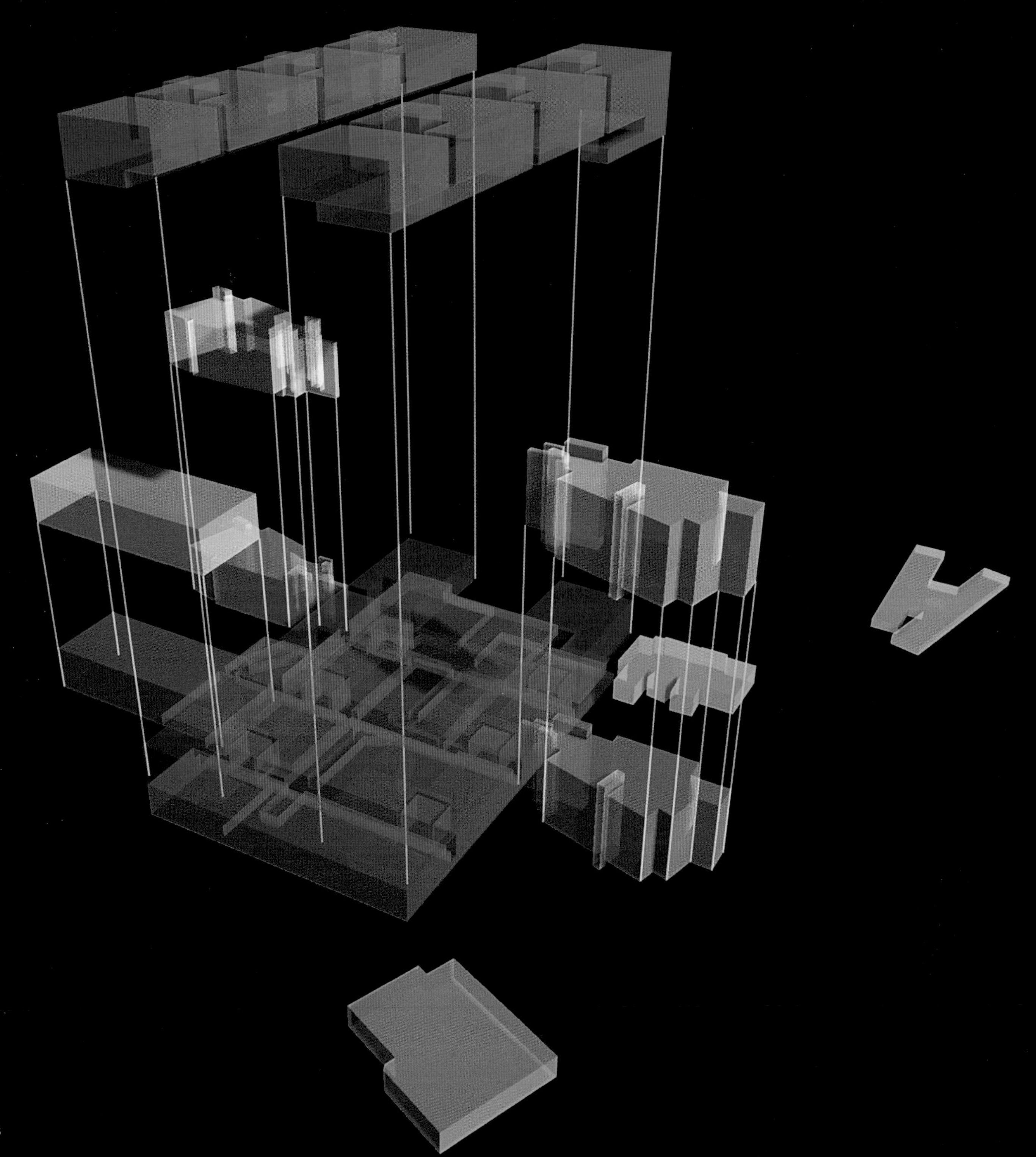

Practising reality

Practising reality: accepting the actual conditions of your surroundings and realistically attainable objectives.
Necessity pushes us to act regardless of the deed or its costs in the conviction that any 'miserable piece of land' may harbour emotions, sensations, images, sounds, smells and ideas. But if the ideas are not transformed into reality, do they evaporate?
You can photograph reality, take it out of its context and extract (surgically?) its components or maybe entire sections. Then you transplant them to a new site and there they take on new life and different, though still interesting, meanings. Record with imagination, using intuition and discussion, context and abstraction, conservation and innovation.
It is certainly not a question of art but the desire to build ideas based on a budget, often using low quality technology and a permanent shortfall of experience.
Strength is in action, ethics in reason.
You always try to make clear the theme of the project but projects can be disassembled like the layers of a drawing. This too is one of the conditions you have to accept: it is easier to isolate a problem in order to think about it, discuss it and resolve it. Our city is exponential in its capacity to create new languages and realities.
Any project has to compromise with reality but not compromise its logic.

Housing, Altare

Altare City Council
Residential buildings
Period: 1996 - in progress

Two rows of houses line the provincial road with space on the sides of the hill behind for single family and two-family houses. The roads are set in a grid pattern that forms the basis of part of the project.

The conventional form of the buildings with double-sided sloping roofs is contrasted by the alternating of pierced volumes and use of untraditional materials.

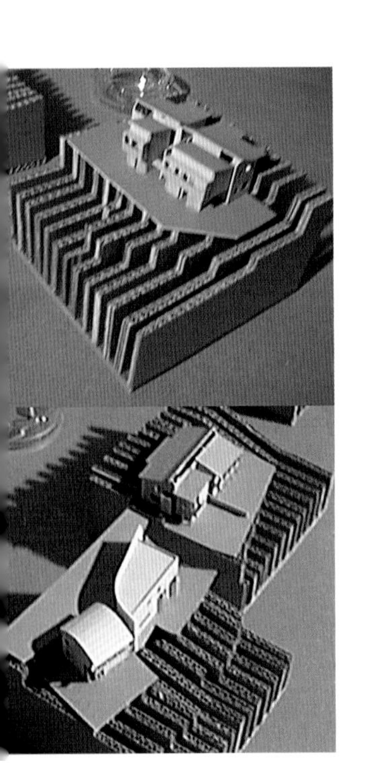

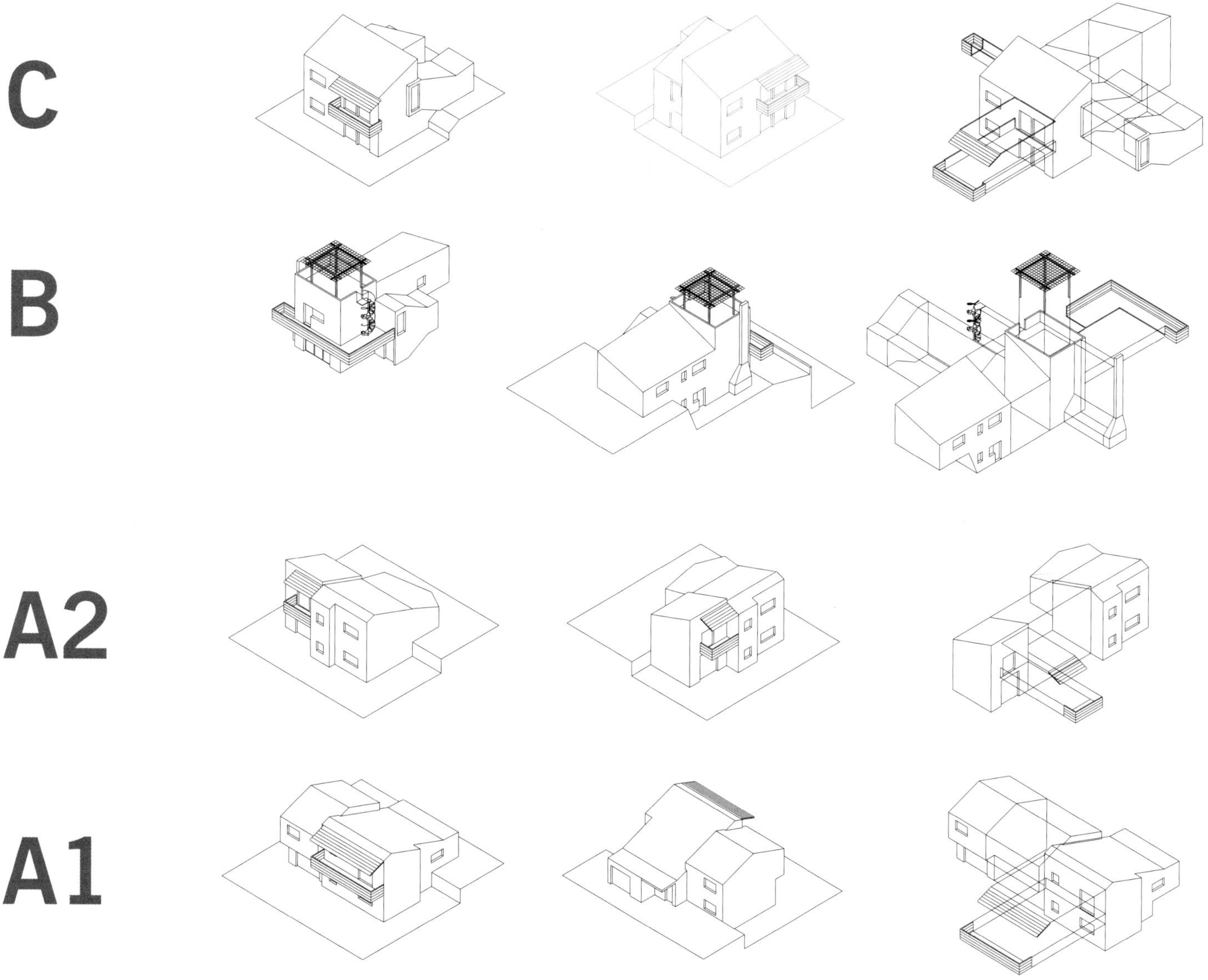

C

B

A2

A1

JuventuStadium

Juventus FC spa
Competition for the new JuventuStadium
to seat 34,000 spectators
Period: competition 1998

The new stadium has been conceived as a theatre for football and designed on the basis of a programme specified by Juventus. The criteria of the design were excellent visibility, comfort, the playing field itself, lighting and aeration.

The project is also a prototype in that it allows the requirements of other sporting companies to be developed within an entertainment area offering facilities for fitness, shops, theme restaurants etc.

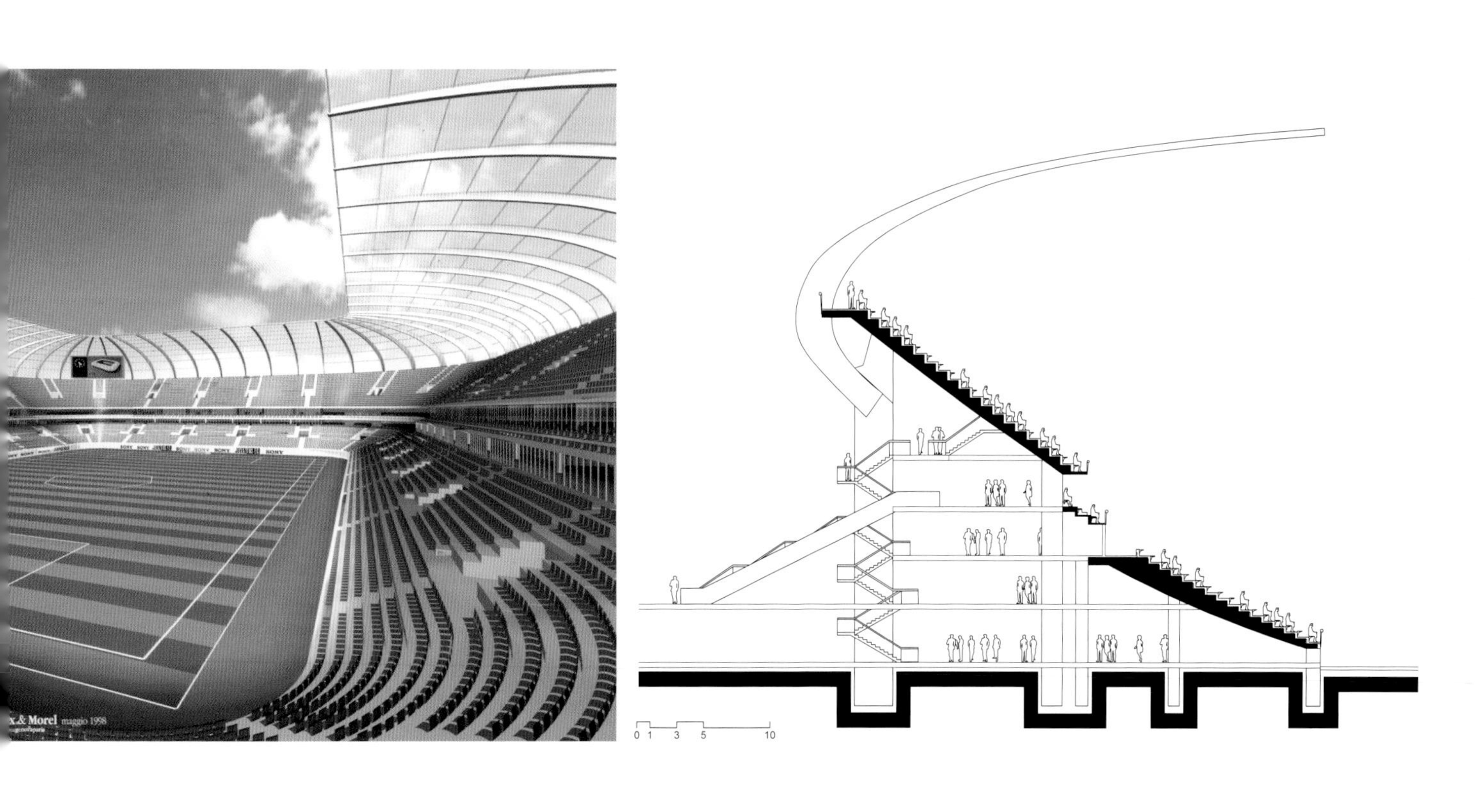
x & Morel maggio 1998
0 1 3 5 10

Thermal complex, Santo Domingo

Terme di Saturnia spa
New thermal centre
2000 - in progress

The physical dimensions and context of the project have permitted a design that emphasises the spa nature of the site and the surrounding nature. The complex slowly dissolves into smaller elements as it moves towards the flat area and divides the common areas from the private sections on different levels.

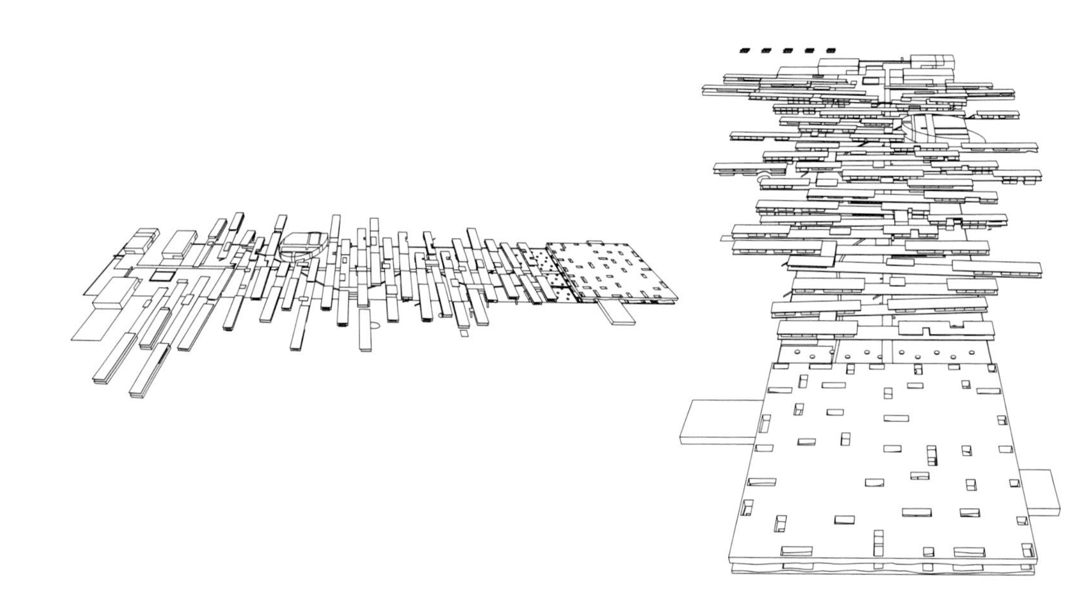

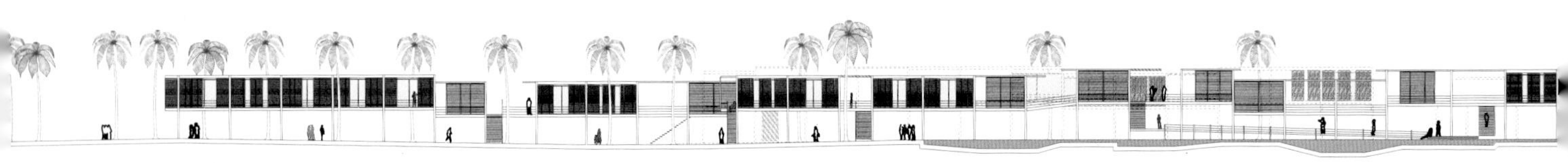

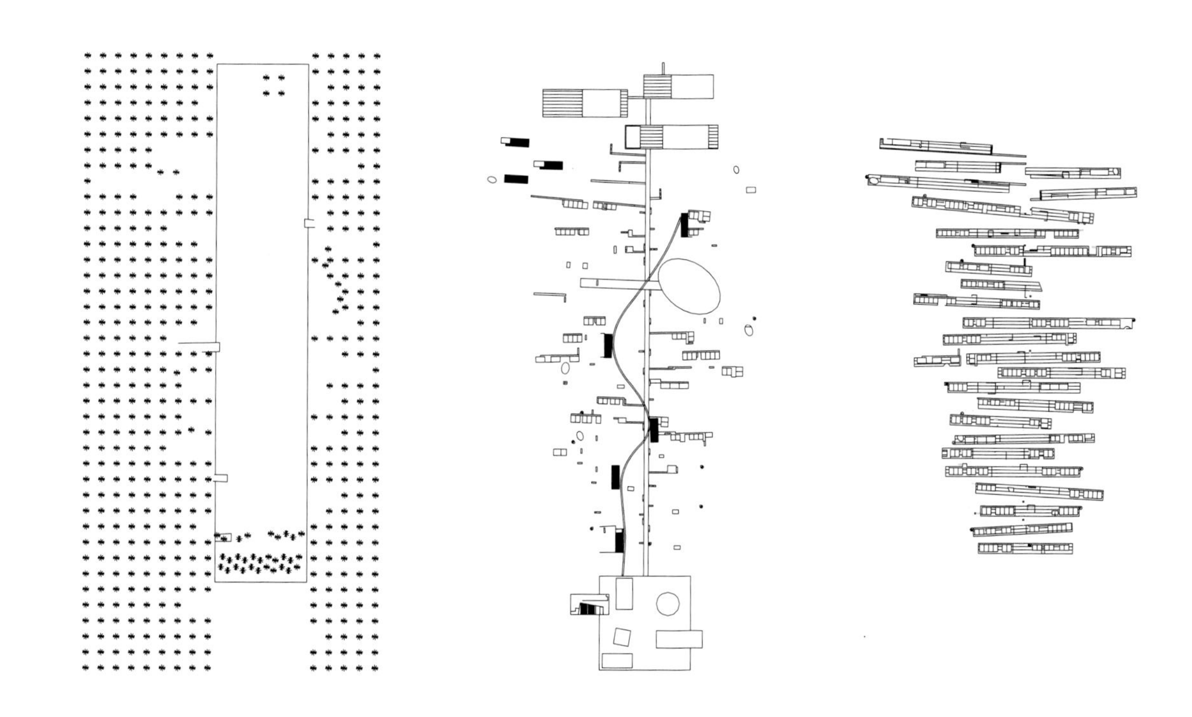

Children's convalescent home, Alba

Children's convalescent home (80 beds)
Period: 2000 - in progress

The lovely natural environment of the hills of Piedmont forms the setting and challenge for a 'natural' design of a convalescent home for children suffering from cardiopathic disturbances. The setting and final users themselves form the starting point for the principal decisions to be made: expansion of the farming 'structure', and division and arrangement of the various sections into common and private areas.

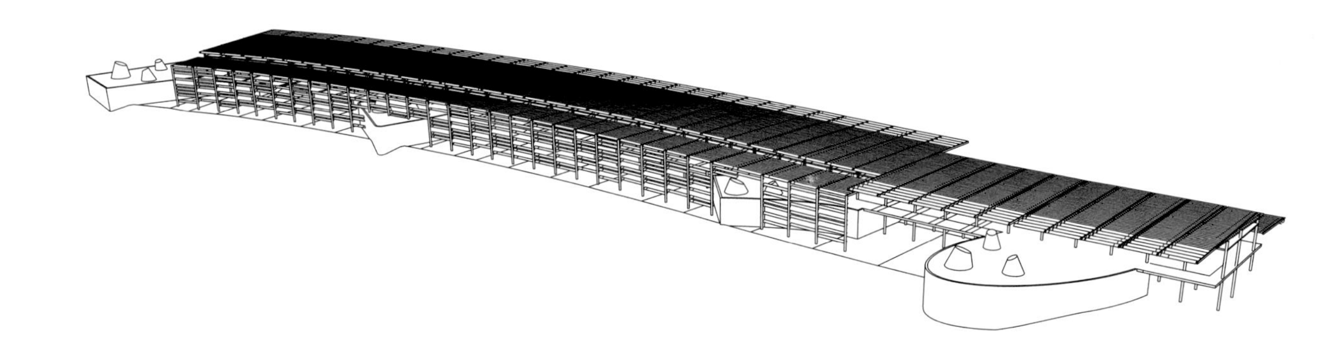

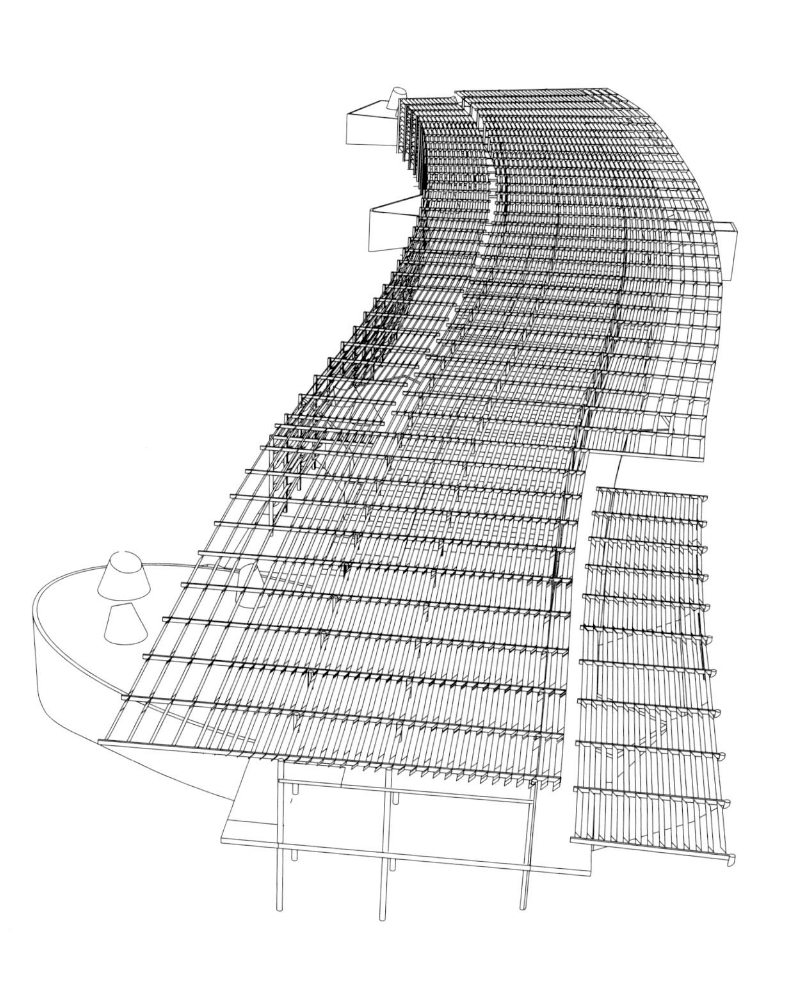

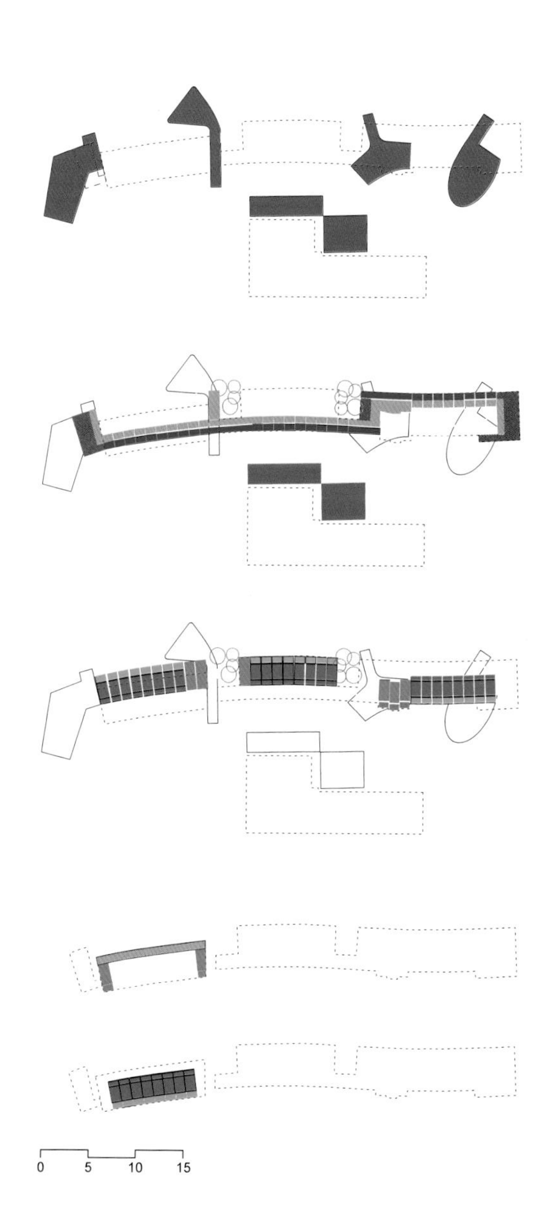
0
5
10
15

Vertical development, renovation, replacement. Three projects in progress

Bossarino, Vado Ligure
Superintendency of Public Works Liguria
Period: 1999/2000 - in progress

An office building in Vado Ligure, the renovation and adaptation of a building to be used for university laboratories in Genoa, and the new centre of the Financial Police in Albenga are three ongoing projects that are based on similar volumes but which differ in their aims and approaches: vertical development (Vado Ligure), alteration and renovation of an existing structure (Genoa), and replacement (Albenga) offer contrasts and points of debate.

New Bossarino offices
in Vado Ligure

Renovation of university
laboratories, Genoa

Financial Police building
in Albenga

In search of freedom, inequality and responsibility

The list on the right stands for the need to introduce rules that hold architectural elements together without too much involvement and without reducing the debate to diatribes between different schools, factions and/or powers.
The list on the left represents freedom and irregularity but also responsibility.
We feel our position is on the left of the page: our duty is to ask ourselves not how a building is made but why it is made in a particular way. It's important to tackle the political function of the design where 'political function' is understood to mean architectural militancy, i.e. the ability to deform an institution-function; the meaning of the building with reference to this ability; the ability to say no; and the inevitable and composed emotional violence of the project imposed on the user.

Collage
Synthetic (chemical)
Fashion
Before and after
Difference
Institute
School
Speech
Forms
History
Tradition

Old and new
Courage
Technology
Elements
Free combination
Context, place, meaning, interior
Crisis
Economy
Pollution

Institute
Anarchy
Art
Paper
Clarity
City
Collage
Complexity?
Competition
Comparison
Context, place, meaning, interior
Contradiction?
Courage
Knowledge
Critical knowledge
Crisis

Critics
Culture
Difference
Doubt, doubt, doubt, …

Critics
Knowledge
Critical knowledge
Ethics
Culture
Project
Identity
Theory
Reflection
Ideas
Paper
Competition
Profession
Myths
Anarchy
Mondo
Insolence
Serenity
Composedness
Impression
Emotion
Urban
Freaks

Economy
Elements
Emotion
Ethics
Event
Forms
Futures!
Future
Future?
Designer name
Group
Ideas
Identity
Imagination
Impression
Pollution
Insolence
Free combination
Speech
Demonstration
Subject
Mediterraneanness
Profession

Demonstration
Event
Dream
School
Transparency
Subject
Box
Complexity ?
Policy
Contradiction?
Art
City
Future
Imagination
Present
Public space
Open space
Space
Style
Designer name

Future?
Futures!

Myths
Fashion
Mondo
Freaks
Birth
Countryside
Present
Before and after
Policy
Project
Project
Schedule?
Reflection
Reflection
Rugged
Box
School
School
Serenity
Synthetic (chemical)
Dream
Survival

Survival
Birth
Clarity
Spontaneity
Reflection
Schedule?
Urban?
Territory!
Countryside?
Mediterranean
Mediterraneanness
Rugged
Group
Project
Comparison
Violence
Doubt, doubt, doubt, …

Space
Open space
Public space
Spontaneity
Style
History
Technology
Theory
Territory!
Tradition
Composedness
Transparency
Transparency?
Urban
Urban?
Old and new
Violence

Opera House, Cardiff

International restricted design competition, 1994

An opera theatre to be built close to the sea in a superb panoramic and urban setting.

Two large curtains that open and close independently; the curtain on the stage indicates the start of the performance, while the one that hides and protects the glass shell of the tiers opens like a huge eyelid to look over the city and the port.

Attention is drawn to the movement of individuals within the theatre, creating a performance within a performance, and so offering a variant on the traditional horse-shoe design.

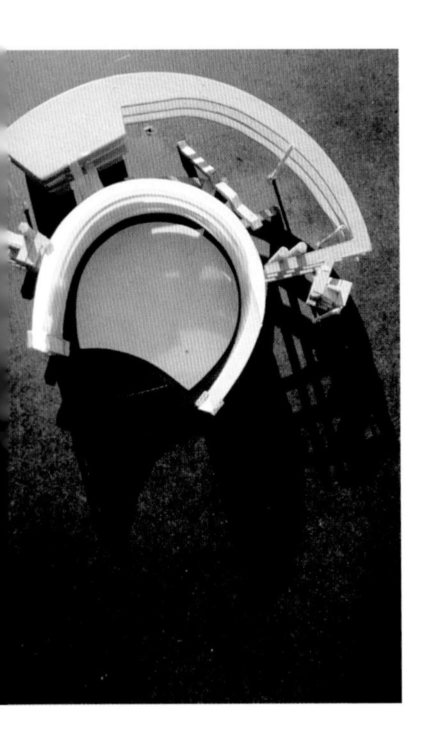

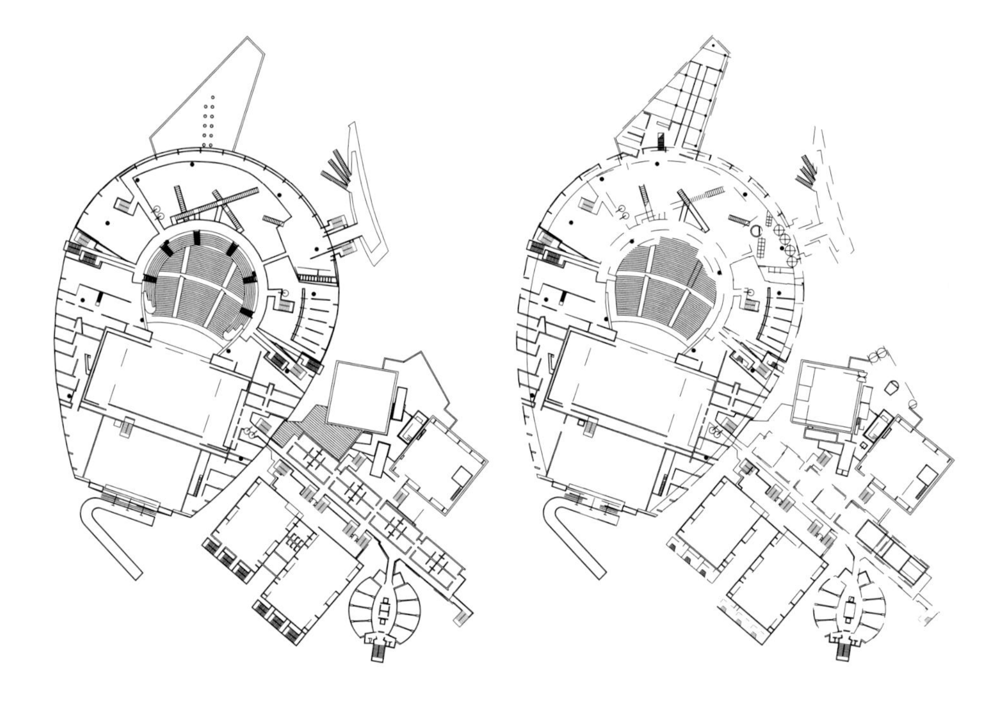

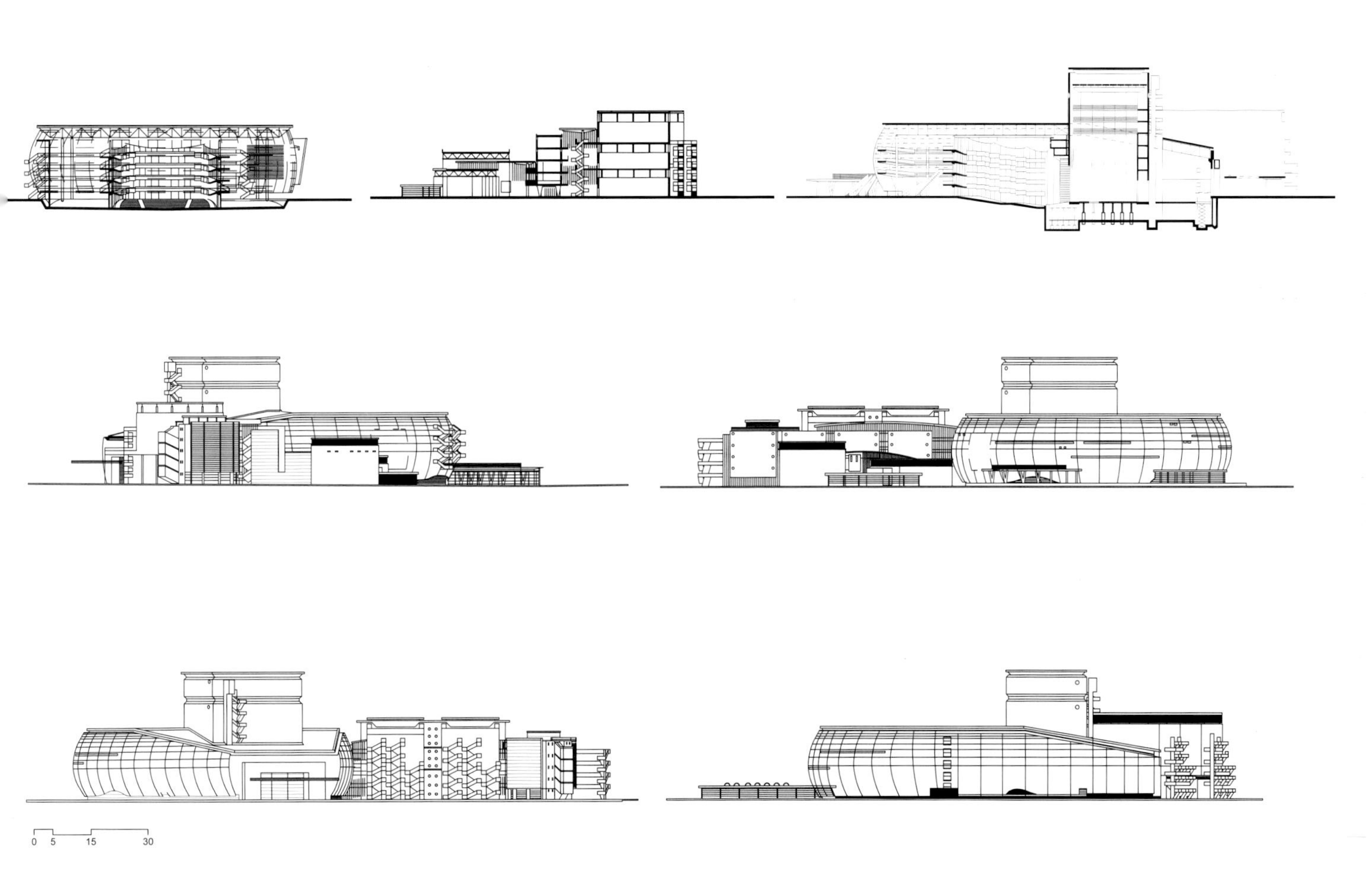
0 5 15 30

Expansion of the Law Courts, Siena

International restricted design competition, 2000

The idea behind the current Law Courts building was its position at the edge of the space between the built-up area enclosed by the walls and the green open area known as Lizza Park.

The 5+1 proposal was motivated by the desire to strengthen the values of the existing building in an already strongly characterised area:

- dialogue with the city walls (not just as an enclosure but also as an element that contributes to the city's current form) that belong and give identity to the city; architecturally, this dialogue has been created by the use of brickwork in the facade and passageway.

- design of the section in the relationship between the old and the new buildings, as a method of dating and building the city (in the project this was achieved in the connection and distribution between the two buildings).

- the creation of a relationship between the public building and urban spaces that is particularly strong and traditional in Siena (see the Campo and Palazzo Pubblico, Piazza del Duomo and the Cathedral and the Spedale); in the project, this was resolved in the continuity of the relationship between Lizza Park, the existing building and the expansion as far as the public, U-shaped facade on Via Diaz.

Cross section of the foyer

Plan of the foyer

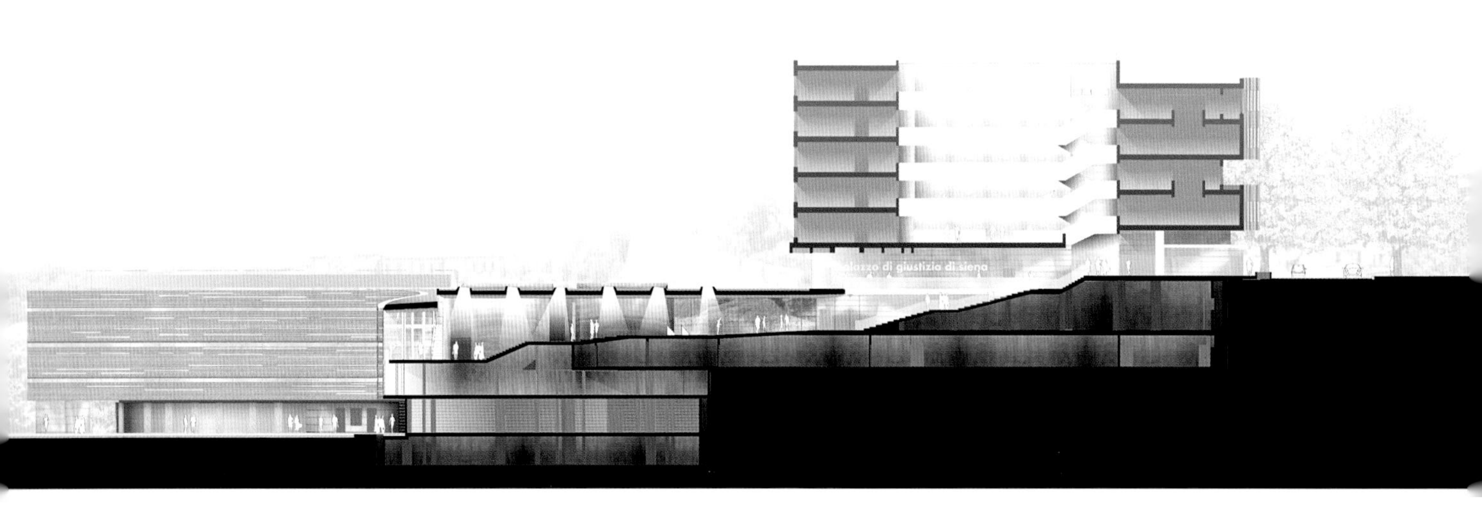

0
5
10

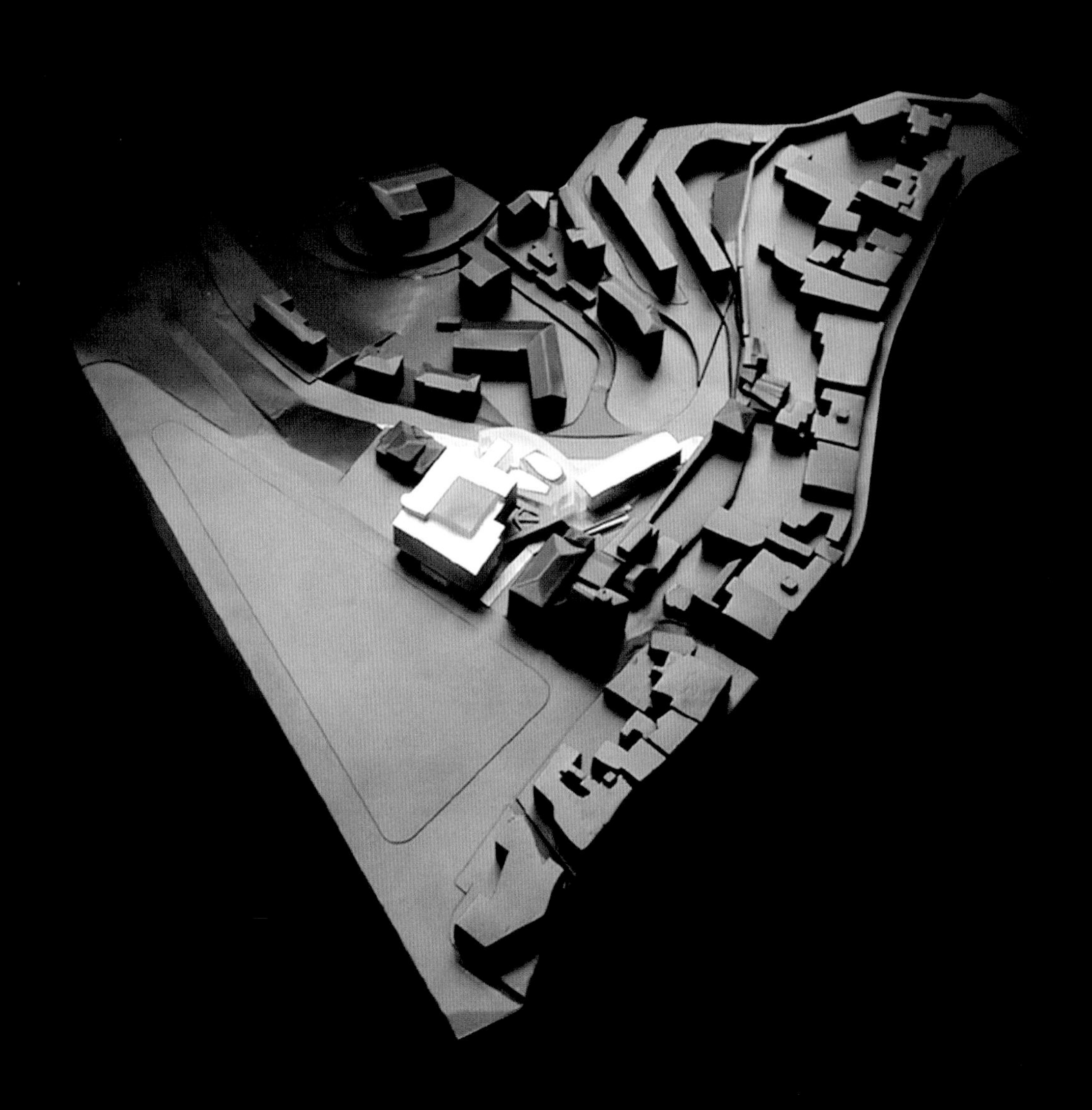

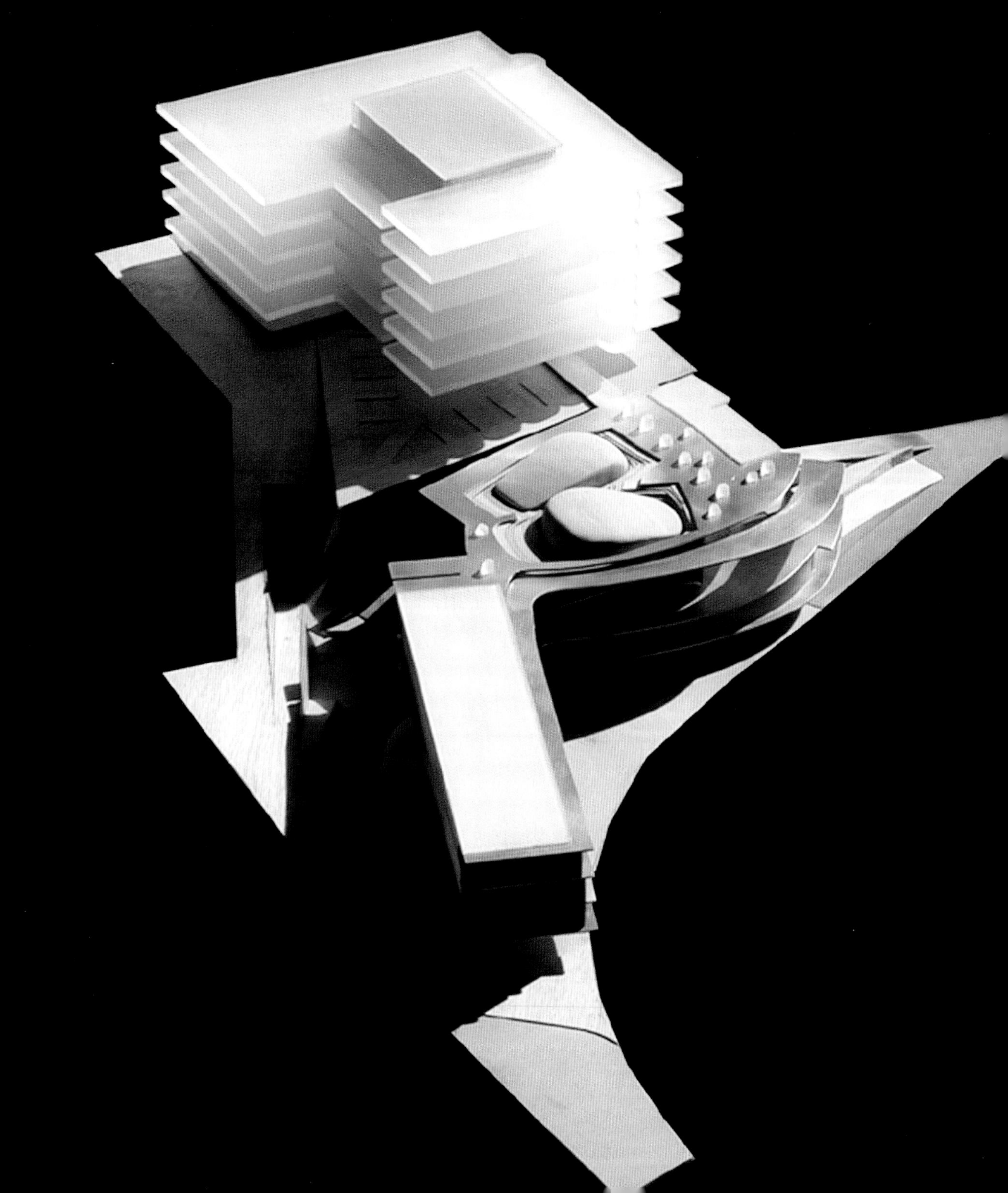

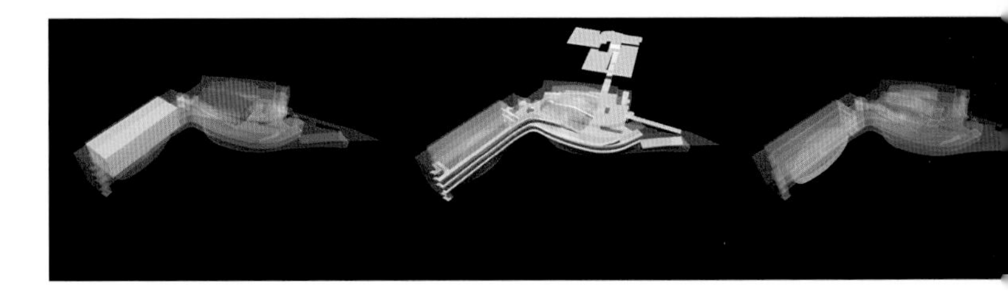

Cross section
of the Courts

Model: the Courts
and distribution system

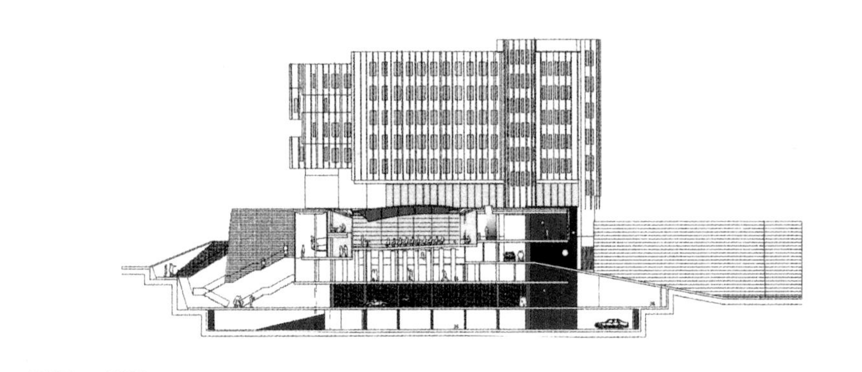

Cross section of the Public
Prosecutor's Office

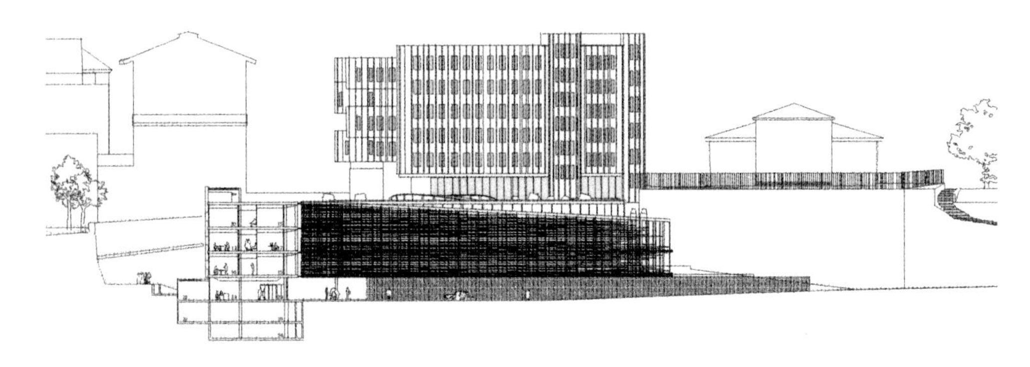

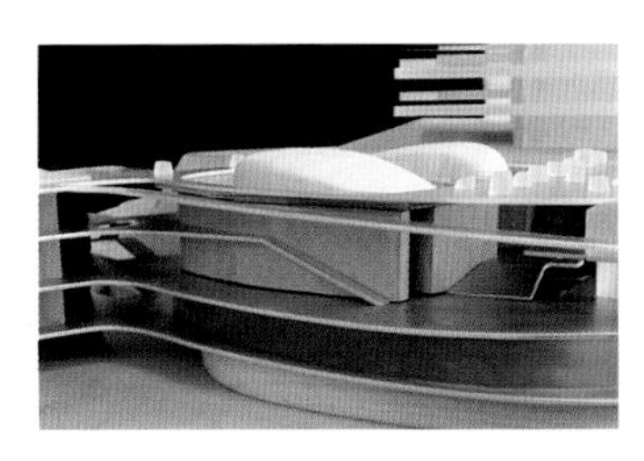

View from Via Diaz

Plan with Via Diaz

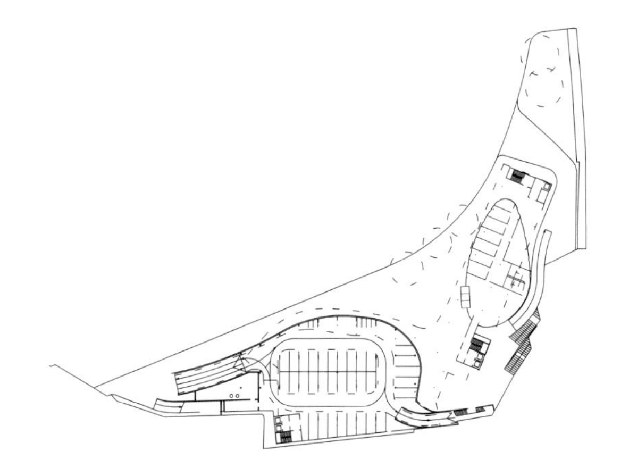

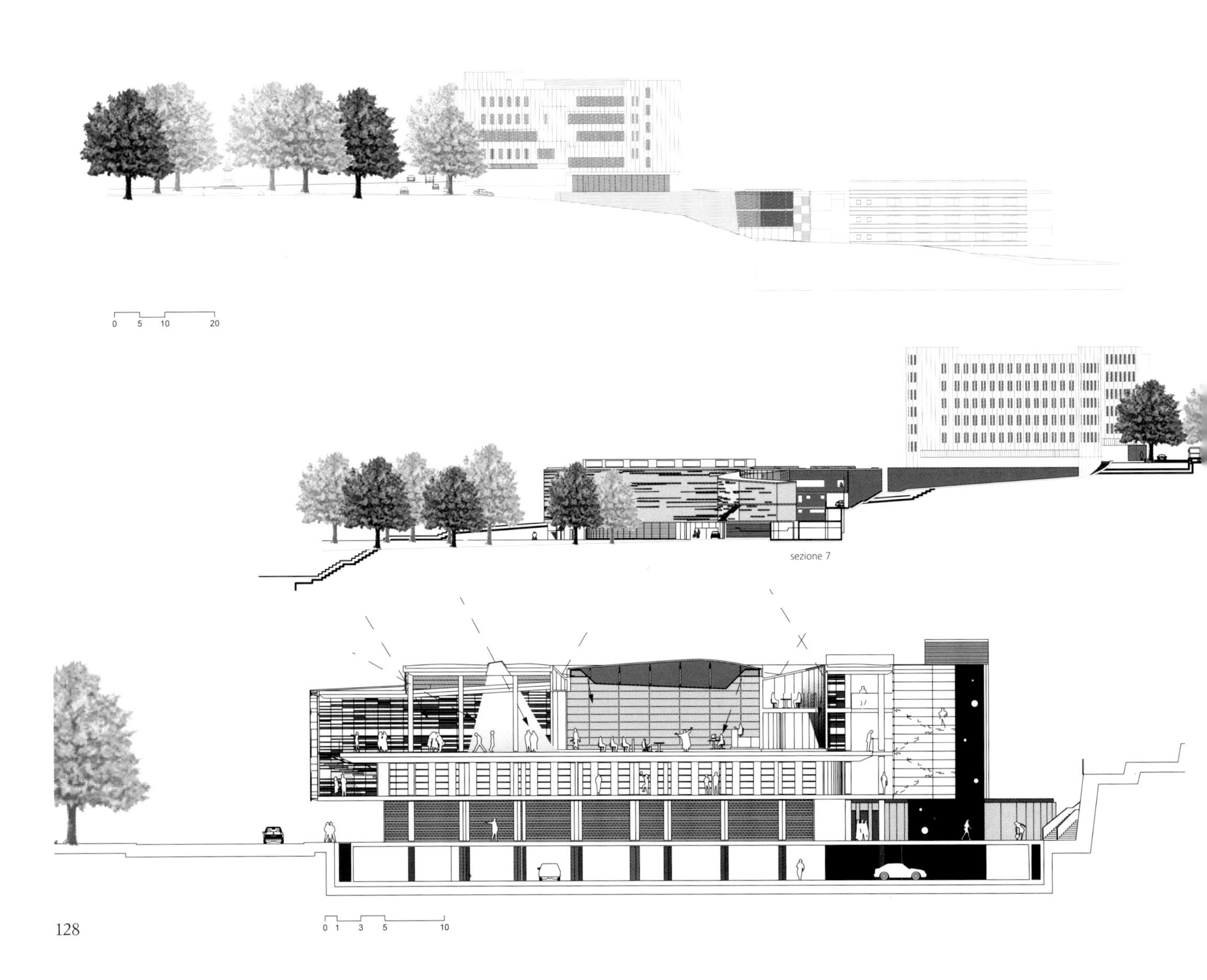
0 5 10 20
sezione 7
0 1 3 5 10

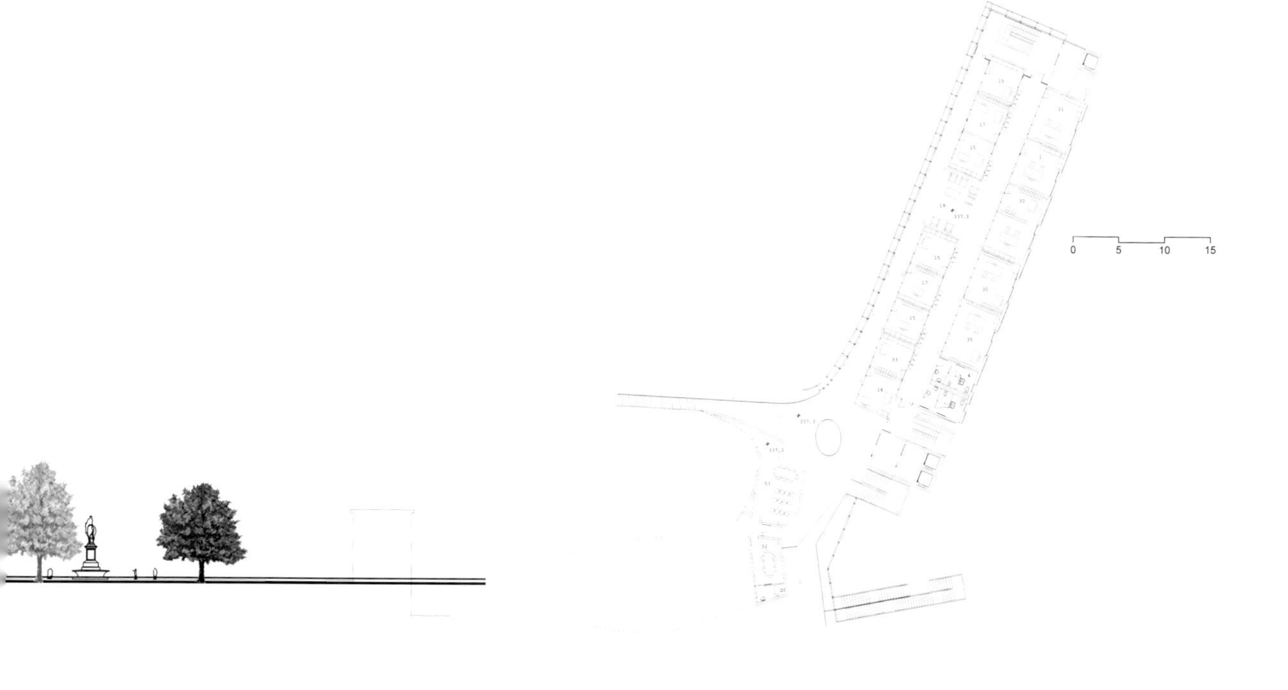
0
5
10
15

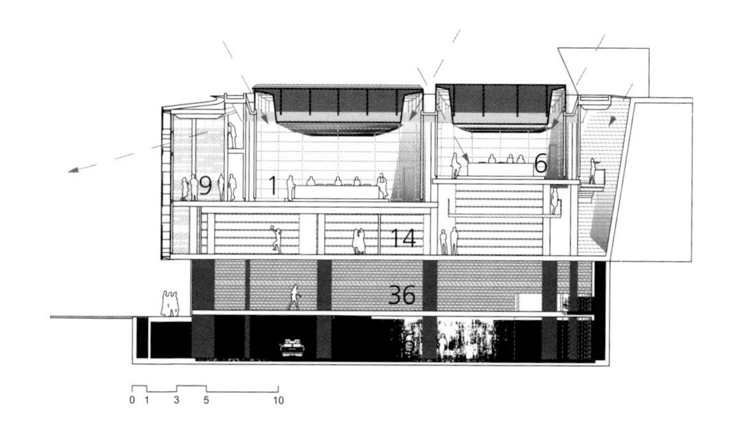
9
1
6
14
36
0 1 3 5 10

The Congress Bridge, Rome

International restricted design competition, 2000

The shadow of ideas

The bridge will not strike the observer with the dramatic beauty of its structure nor with the solidity of its ancient counterparts. The exceptional qualities of this bridge will be found in its attempt to minimise the use of materials and the drain on the territory's resources, and in its inner strength and sensuality.

The design is based on an innovative and highly reduced use of materials and on a non-invasive relationship with its natural and man-made setting by means of sections underground, few ramps or piers, and a continuity between the suspended parts, the underground parts and the co-planar zones.

What will be unique is the bridge's hidden soul.

Hidden soul

The bridge's sensual and hidden power is to be found in the strength of its material.

The attraction of its span and vicinity is derived from the muscular, nervous strength of its ultra high resistant concrete.

The plasticity and hydrometry of this mate-

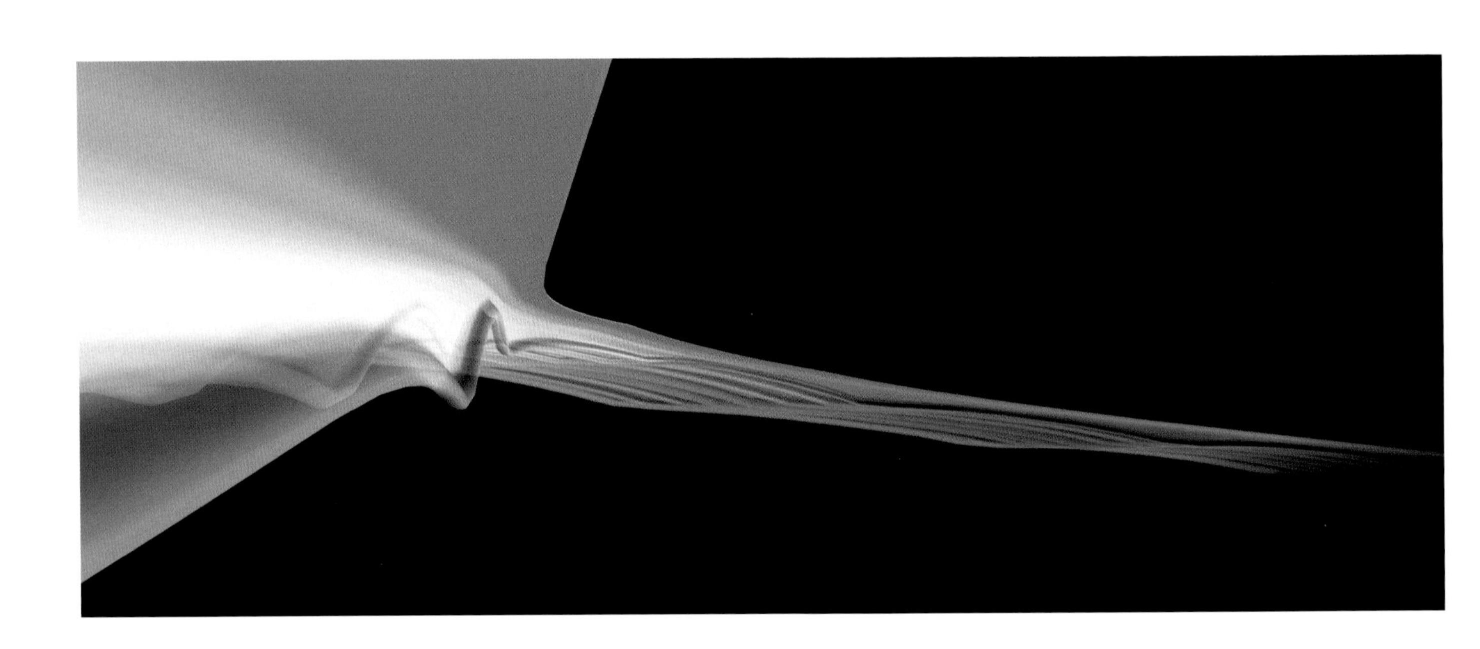

rial allow blends to be made that result in different tactile experiences. The surface is not brutal or heroic but sensual like skin.

The muscular-nervous strength of a slender section of the material is like the strength of the abdomen, or like the sinews in the hand that contract when you take something with the tips of your fingers. The action of supporting the palm of the hand with the tension of the sinews of the back of the hand facing downwards is tactile and 'Mediterranean', as opposed to the 'Anglo-Saxon' technology of the tendons-stays that lift, deforming the knuckles that rise to form spars and impose themselves on the setting. The strength is hidden, almost passive, and awaits the slow passing of the curious along the river bank; only then will its systematic metal geometry of the unbroken series of vigorous arches that emerge from the pillars be truly appreciated.

The perceptional pleasure of its span

The decision to divide the two bridges was based on perception.

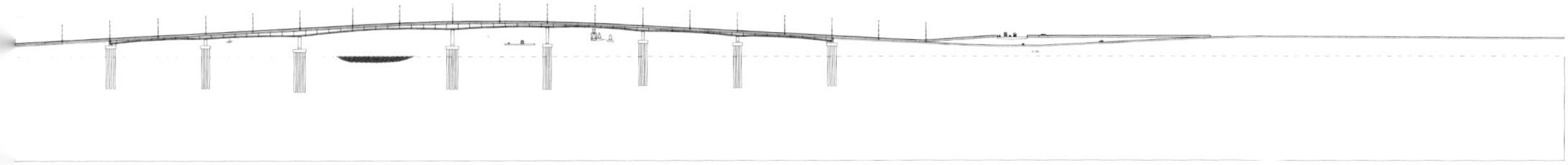

velodromo
viale egeo
viale dell'oceano indiano
cotral
fiume tevere
via del mare
casale tor di valle

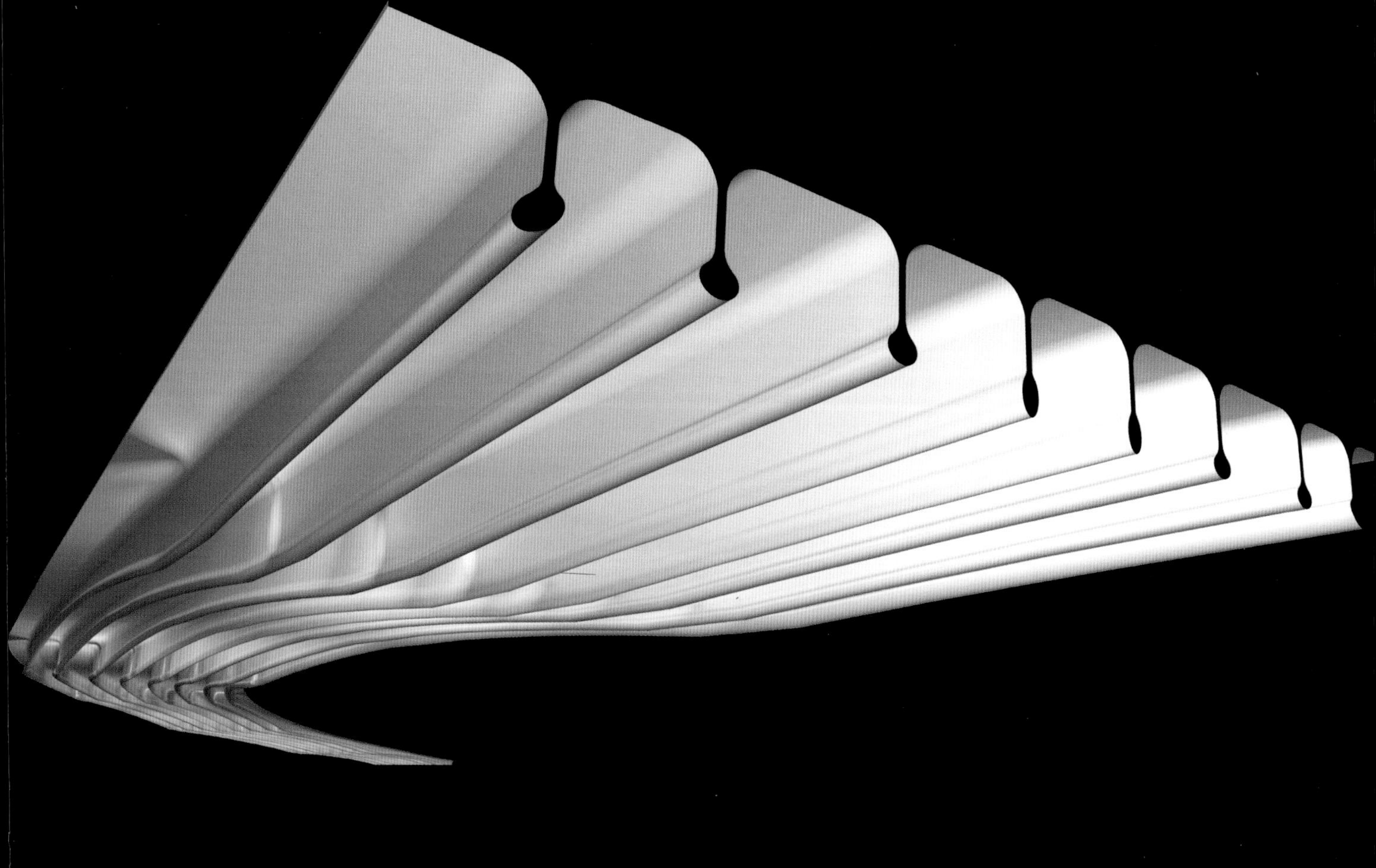

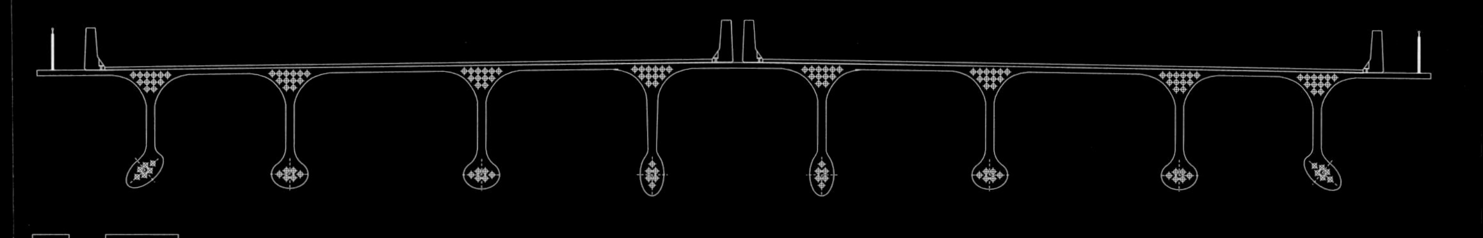
0
1
2
4

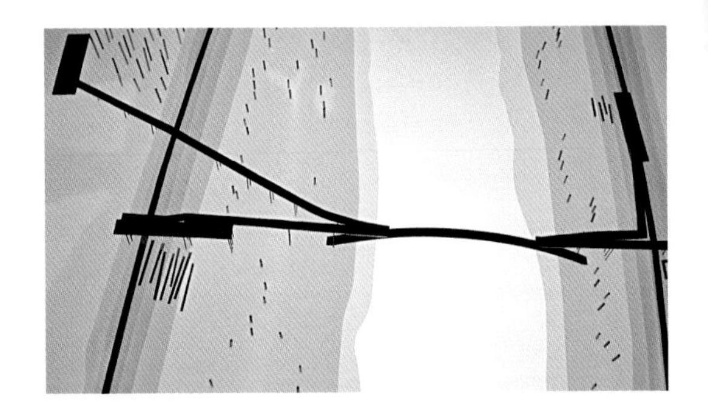

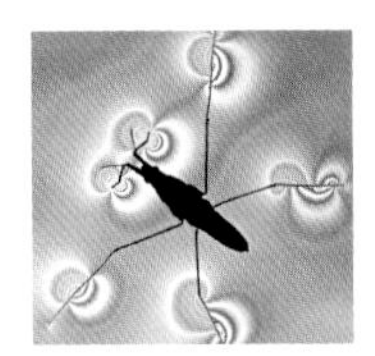

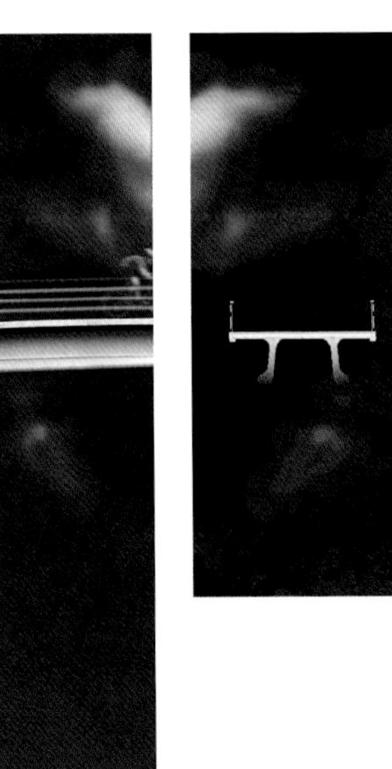

The carriageway:
longitudinal section

The footbridge:
cross section; longitudinal
view; general model

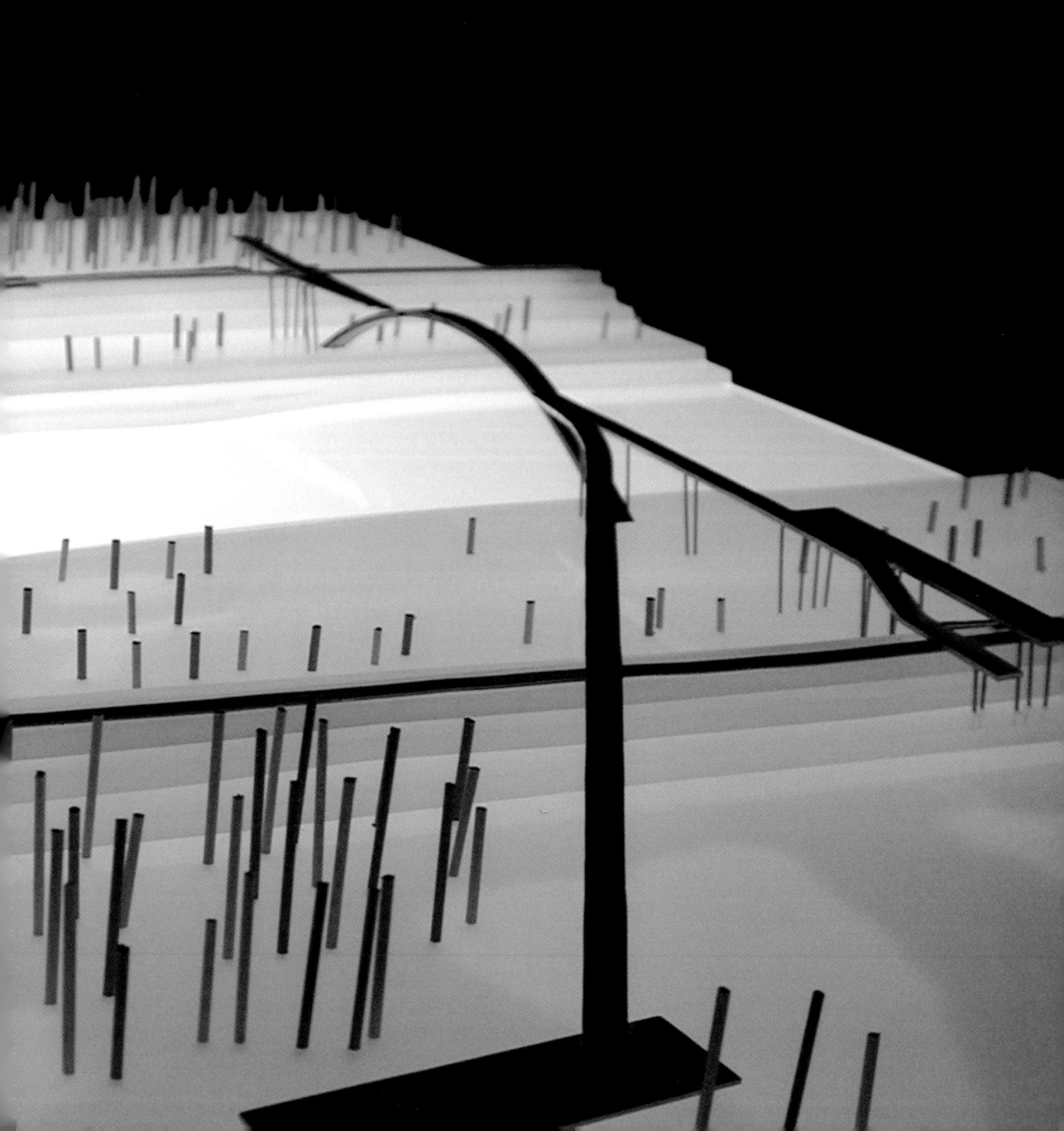

Yves Nacher

Quantum ethics

I have always tended to distrust books about architecture and this distrust does not lessen with increasing age. About three years ago, when 5+1 were still in their early days, they prepared an exhibition in Paris with an accompanying catalogue. I had already told them to forget the idea and to concentrate on their work instead, as the mounting of a self-congratulatory retrospective at such an early stage of development constituted a risk that could have deprived them of any future. I had even written it... in the above-mentioned and censured catalogue (when it comes to friendship, loyalty sometimes pardons you for being inconsistent).

Now they are at it again and here I am writing these lines — oh well, we are what we are and there's nothing we can do about it. In the first place, I still think that a monograph before being as old as Philip Johnson is overhasty (though, if you've reached Philip Johnson's age, rather pressing), or perhaps somewhat presumptuous unless one has good reasons for exhibiting oneself in all senses of the word.

Three years ago I found reasons to go along with 5+1 in this business about the exhibition: they were risk-takers in the architectural debate when every debate in Italy was prohibited; they crucified the upper echelons of the university system that was only concerned with ensuring its own survival through the production of clones in their own image; they shot down the magnates who monopolised positions of power in inverse proportion to their talent; and their outlook on architecture was the same as MTV's attitude to zapping. In short, they were a little like David wading into a sea of Goliaths. Since then, many things have changed. The world of architecture in Italy has opened up (a little), the list of their commissions has lengthened, they have had the courage to tackle programmes whose complexity and breadth have raised the envy of more than a few, and they have had the gumption to have had one of their constructions inaugurated by the President of Italy. That's more than development, it's a quantum leap.

I am writing this 'blind', without knowing what the book contains. That is why I asked to be able to add an afterword, so as to invite the reader to reflect on the previous pages, so that he might discern 5+1's shift towards 'adulthood', their passage to 'serious work' that has rendered my fears of their premature self-appreciation unfounded. I asked this favour with trust (because mine is impeccable) and with affection (ditto) but, as I have always been rather paternalistic, I asked it anyway.

Appendix

Chronology

Paola Arbocò (Genova, 1965)
Pierluigi Feltri (Savona, 1962)
Alfonso Femia (Taurianova, 1966)
Gianluca Peluffo (Savona, 1966)
Maurizio Vallino (Genova, 1967)

1995
The 5+1 studio of associated architects was established in Genoa by five graduates of the Faculty of Architecture at Genoa University where they worked on architectural design courses with Enrico D. Bona.
They put together the book *A Carnevale anche i grattacieli ballano. Ancora 106 frammenti sulla città di New York*, with Luca Forno, published by Joshua.

1996
They won the first prize in a national competition regarding the signalling system at Campi industrial park in Genoa.
They published the book *Francia 2013 - Italia 10. Non si uccide anche così l'architettura? Note, commenti e suggestioni a margine dei concorsi di architettura* edited by Joshua. Since 1997 they have been the editors of a new series of books, 'JA', with the collaboration of Yves Nacher.
They won the design competition for the new hospital in Biella.

1997
Since 1997 they have been part of the IFYA (International Forum of Young Architects), and in the same year they were commissioned by Spes spa to convert the former Bligny Barracks in Savona into a new university campus.

1998
They were invited by the Italian Institute for Culture in Paris to expound on the creative process in an exhibition entitled *5+1 associati: progetti in gruppo. Fin qui tutto bene* with a catalogue jointly published with Joshua.

1999
They won a bid to design the new archaeological centre in Aquileia.
In the same year they took part in the Biennale dei Giovani Artisti dell'Europa e del Mediterraneo held in Rome (May–June) where they displayed their work in the exhibition *Gerico* and a portrait of the studio in 'grande ét@gere'.
They were invited to take part in the second phase of the international design competition for the expansion of the Palace of Justice (Law Courts) in Siena.

2000
They were invited by INARCH to display their work at the Italian Institute of Culture in Prague and at the Venice Biennale, both of which were dedicated to young Italian architects.
They won the competition to construct an office building at Vado Ligure and were invited to take part in the second phase of the international design competition for the new Congress Bridge in Rome.

Works

Public buildings

1997
New hospital centre, Biella, with Enrico D. Bona, Mauro Strata

1998
Conversion of the former Bligny Barracks into a new university campus and multi-purpose centre for business and advanced training, Savona, with Chaix & Morel.
Complex of the Sant'Apollinare Nuovo Basilica, development of Cinema Corso into a multi-purpose hall, welcoming centre in the Mosaics Museum in Theodoric's Palace (restoration of the Basilica, Ravenna), with Claudio Cicchetti

1998–99
Lift system at the Rocca del Castello in San Michele, Cagliari

1998–2000
Visitors' Centre and Antiquarium in Aquileia Forum, with Maurizio Giufré

1999–2000
Reclamation of the former Metalmetron factory area, Savona

1999
Conversion of the former Chimica Industriale buildings into university laboratories and halls, Genoa

2000
Children's convalescent home, Alba, Cuneo, with Claudio Cicchetti, Maurizio Giufré.
Financial Police Administration Centre, Albenga

Housing, office buildings and tourist facilities

1995
New residential complex, Altare, Savona, with Paolo Grenni

1997
Hotel and residences in Alassio, Savona

2000
Barahona thermal complex, Santo Domingo, with Art Design.
Office building, Vado Ligure, Savona

Public spaces

1996
New seaside promenade, Savona, with Fabrizio Feltri, Susanna Feltri, Marta Sperati.
Upgrading of public areas: Piazza Sant'Antonio and Viale Dante in Sestri Levante, with Enrico D. Bona.
New seaside promenade and environmental upgrade, Alassio

1998
Public areas in the old dockyard, Genoa.
Cycle track, green area and public areas in the city centre of Casarza Ligure, Genoa

1998–99
Piazza Assunta and Via Genova, Celle Ligure, with Rudy Ricciotti

Sports buildings and leisure centres

1998
New Juventus stadium, Turin, with Chaix & Morel, Luigi Sobrero

1999
Upgrading of the sports facilities at Rio Cortino, Sori, Genoa

1999–2000
Leisure centre in the former AGL building, San Donato Milanese, with Sebastiano Brandolini, Ottavio Di Blasi, Benedetto Quaquaro

Town-planning projects

1997
Overall upgrade programme of public areas in the historical centres of San Lorenzo, Bocco di Leivi, San Rufino, Garbuggi, Leivi, with Mauro Strata.
Overall upgrade programme of public areas in the historical centres of Riva Levante and Riva Ponente, Sestri Levante

1997–98
Preliminary studies for the town-planning scheme for Genoa port, with Stefano Boeri, Enrico D. Bona, Fabrizio Paone

1998–99
Town-planning scheme of Trieste port with Technital, Marconsult, Stefano Boeri, Fabrizio Paone

1999
Architectural and town-planning projects of the town centre of Sestri Levante, Genoa.
City cycle tracks in Sestri Levante, Genoa

Competitions

First prizes

1996
Signage and co-ordinated image of Campi area, Genoa, national competition, with Marcello Vagge

1999
Cyborg City International Competition: artificial and mechanical islands for New York, international competition, with Michelle Cecchini, Francesca Colombo, Sara De Biasi, Lisa Fellini

2000
Office building, Vado Ligure, Savona

Signage

1997
Organisation of Piazza Modena, Genoa, national competition, third place.
Plan for council houses, Bari, national competition, with Fabiola Minas.
Lungomare dei Ciclopi, Acicastello, national competition, sixth prize, with Fabio Brocai and ZTL

Invitations

2000
Expansion of the Law Courts, Siena, international competition, second phase, with Chaix & Morel, Progest srl, M. Taccini.
Congress Bridge, Rome, international competition,

second phase, with Rudy Ricciotti, Annalaura Spalla, Progest srl, MPS srl.
New university buildings, Bologna, international competition, second phase, with Chaix & Morel.
New Collège 600, Fabrègue-Montpellier, second phase, in collaboration with Rudy Ricciotti (architecte mandataire)

Other competition bids

1995
Opera House, Cardiff, Wales, international competition.
Project for the re-organisation and upgrade of the Prado Museum, Madrid, international competition

1996
Project for the layout of a town block, Dietikon, Switzerland, as part of the Europan international competition

1997
City upgrade project, Thessaloniki, Greece, as part of the Europan international competition.
Urban upgrade project, Grugliasco, Turin, national competition.

Exhibitions

1998
5+1 associati: progetti in gruppo, Italian Cultural Institute, Paris, 2–14 February

1999
Gerico, Biennale dei Giovani Artisti dell'Europa e del Mediterraneo, Rome, June

2000
Gerico 60 (20+20+20) Giovani Architetti Italiani, Chapel of San Carlo Borromeo, Italian Cultural Institute, Prague, 27 March.
La sperimentazione del nuovo. Giovani architetti: un incontro sulla condizione contemporanea, Venice Biennale, 15–16 September

2001
5+1 architetti associati, Genua, GTA, EHT, Zurich, 12 January - 22 March

Conferences

1998
Il sistema dei concorsi in architettura: Italia-Francia a confronto, Genoa, Reggio Emilia, Venice, Turin

1999
Deformazione del reale: progetti di gruppo dello studio 5+1, Turin Polytechnic, Mondovì, January.
Infrastructure et paysage: le territoire 'trans-active': projets et réalisations, École Méditerranéenne des Jardins et du Paysage, Grasse, France, January .
5+1 associati: spiagge urbane e spazi pubblici, Architecture Department, University of Pescara, March.
5+1 associati: progetti in gruppo, Architecture Department, Genoa University and INARCH - Acer, Rome, September–December

2000
Paesaggi urbani, Turin Polytechnic, March

Publications

1994
A Carnevale anche i grattacieli ballano. Ancora 106 frammenti sulla città di New York, with Luca Forno, Joshua, Sestri Levante

1996
Francia 2013 - Italia 10. Non si uccide anche così l'architettura? Note, commenti e suggestioni a margine dei concorsi di architettura, Joshua, Sestri Levante

1997
Genova, spazi pubblici della città, Joshua, Sestri Levante.
Atelier Seraji, Paris. Nasrine Seraji, JA1 series, Joshua, Sestri Levante

1998
Fin qui tutto bene. Jusqu'ici tout va bien, Joshua, Sestri Levante.
Campus in Savona, JA3 series, Joshua, Sestri Levante.
Hérault-Arnod, Grenoble, JA2 series, Joshua, Sestri Levante

Bibliography

1998
'Savone. Des casermes transformées en pôle universitaire', in *Le Moniteur*, no. 4936, 3 July

1999–2000
'5+1', in *Almanacco di Casabella. Giovani architetti italiani 1999-2000*

2000
'Roma 1999 - Sarajevo 2001: Gerico 20+20+20', in *Il progetto*, no. 6, January.
'Qui si impara a gestire il futuro', in *Specchio della Stampa*, no. 225, 20 May.
'Addio alle armi', in *Costruire*, no. 209, October.
'A university takes over the barracks', in *Domus*, no. 831, November.
'De Caserme en Campus', in *L'Arca International*, no. 37, November.
'From the Barracks to the Campus', in *L'Arca*, no. 153, November.
Prove 6. Museo di Aquileia, Edicom, Venezia

2001
'5+1 uguale fantasia', in *Costruire*, no. 212, January

List of collaborators

In 2000

Pietro Bruzzone
Andrea Capurro
Simonetta Cenci
Dahlia De Macina
Marinella Maggi
Gabriele Maria Pulselli
Emma Ruggieri
Sara Traverso

CAD, computer rendering
Luca Bonsignorio
Andrea Di Mauro
Stefano Fragola
Enrico Martino
Antonio Terranova
Paolo Vassallo

Graphic design
Francesca Ameglio

Models
Daniele Marchetti
Luca Pozzi
Ilaria Sisto

Video and web
Sergio Tani

Since 1995

Antonio Lagorio
(until 1999)
Christian Benvenuto
Andrea Bonello
Chiara Braida
Serena Breschi
Alessia Colli
Laura Devoti
Giovanni Guerrieri
Uwe Hellwig
Peter Klaus
Fabiola Minas
Francesca Muzio
Gilberto Palladino
Luca Petrucci
Nicoletta Piersantelli
Raffaella Pirrello
Nicola Pisani
Chiara Poggi
Felix Rahne
Giacomo Razeto
Stefano Scorza
Marco Sinesi
Jochen Stein
Cristina Troilo
Davide Zanoletti

Photographic credits

Ernesta Caviola;
Rossella Murgia (p. 145);
Emanuele Piccardo (pp. 29, 32, 33, 34, 35, 36, 37);
Flavio Stagnaro (pp. 24 bottom left, 43 bottom, 64, 65, 68 top centre, 70);
Stefano Golberg (pp. 104, 105); 5+1 archive

5+1 thanks

Paolo Amadio, Sergio Acquilino, Laura Arbocò, Mario Antonio Arnaboldi, Aldo Aymonino, Maurizio e Federica Bagnasco, Marc Baraness, Fabrizio Barbano, François Barré, Fabia Begliomini, Monica Bellucci, Chiara Beria D'Argentine, Federico Berruti, Alessandro Berta, Valerio Bianchi, Matteo Bo, Franco Bocchieri, Walter Bodrato, Massimo Bordone, Dominique Boudet, Angelo Bugatti, Luciano Campagnolo, Rita Capezzuto, Elena Cardani, Francesco Careri, Marco Casamonti, Cesare M. Casati, Ernesta Caviola, Ruth Cawker, Simone Cellesi, Antonio Cenci, Mario Chella, Claudio Cicchetti, Giovanni Corrado, Pietro Corsi, Ugo De Bernardi, Aldo De Poli, Ottavio Di Blasi, Rita, Fabrizio e Susanna Feltri, Marianna, Giusy, Vincenzo e Salvatore Femia, Cesare Ferrero, Giorgio Gatti, Enzo Giammetta, Francesco Ghio, Alessandra Ghisleri, Paolo Grenni, Carlo Guglielminetti, Isabel Hérault, Richard Ingersoll, Stefano La Cava, Marco Lanata, Armando Magliotto, Marco Malaspina, Angelo Massucco, Andrea Meirana, Stefano Migliaro, Jean-Paul Morel, Marco Mulazzani, Rossella Murgia, Pierluigi Mutti, Ondina Norcini, Aldo Norsa, Paolo Oliva, Antonio Pagano, Marco Pascucci, Matilde, Giovanni e Paolo Peluffo, Massimo Perazzo, Luciano Peri, Alain Philip, Emanuele Piccardo, Franz Prati, Benedetto Quaquaro, Monica Racic, Luciana Ravanel, Gabriele Re, Marcella Rebecchini, Stefano Rissetto, Alessandro Rocchi, Tullio Russo, Livio Sacchi, Guendalina Salimei, Massimo Scarpat, Emma Serra, Luciano Siciliano, Paolo Simonetti, Luigi Sobrero, Antonio Solari, Annalaura Spalla, Enea Spini, Giordano Stabile, Flavio Stagnaro, Mauro Strata, Deyan Sudjic, Jacopo Tabarelli, Marco Taccini, Mirco Tardio, Marco Trisciuoglio, Marcello Vagge, Paolo Valentino, Carla e Gio.Batta Vallino, Maurizio Varagnolo, Vito Vattuone, Sandra Venturi, Franco Zagari, Fabrizio Zeba